OCR

British Depth Study 1939–1975

ROSEMARY REES

HODDER
EDUCATION
AN HACHETTE UK COMPANY

ACKNOWLEDGEMENTS

The author and Publishers would like to thank Rob Bircher and Dan Lyndon for their contributions.

Photo credits

Cover *l* London Transport Museum, *c* Michael Webb/Getty Images, *r* Terrence Spencer/Time Life Pictures/Getty Images; **p.4** Vicky/*Evening Standard*, 19 May 1959/British Cartoon Archive, University of Kent, www.cartoons.ac.uk; **p.8** Roger-Viollet/ Topfoto – TopFoto.co.uk; **p.12** Reg Speller/Getty Images; **p.15** Solo Syndication/Associated Newspapers Ltd/By permission of Llyfrgell Genedlaethol Cymru/The National Library of Wales; **p.17** Popperfoto/Getty Images; **p.19** Harry Thompson/Hulton Archive/Getty Images; **p.21** *tl* National Motor Museum/HIP/TopFoto, *tc*, *tr*, *bl*, *bc* & *br* Image courtesy of The Advertising Archives; **p.23** *l* Popperfoto/Getty Images, *r* David Cairns/Stringer/Getty Images; **p.25** Clive Limpkin/Stringer/Getty Images; **p.26** Cummings/Express Syndication/British Cartoon Archive, University of Kent, www.cartoons.ac.uk; **p.27** *b* Jon/*Daily Mail* August 1968/British Cartoon Archive, University of Kent, www.cartoons.ac.uk, *t* Illingworth/*Daily Mail* April 1964/British Cartoon Archive, University of Kent, www.cartoons.ac.uk; **p.28** Jurgen Schadeberg/Getty Images; **p.30** *l* The National Archives/HIP/ TopFoto, *c* & *r* Image courtesy of The Advertising Archives; **p.33** Roger-Viollet/Topfoto; **p.34** Image courtesy of The Advertising Archives; **p.35** *Evening Standard*/Getty Images; **p.39** Image courtesy of The Advertising Archives; **p.40** Topham Picturepoint, TopFoto.co.uk; **p.43** Image courtesy of The Advertising Archives; **p.51** Topfoto; **p.57** Mirrorpix; **p.59** Topfoto; **p.63** *t* Mirrorpix, *b* Hulton-Deutsch Collection/CORBIS; **p.64** *l* Cummings/Express Syndication/ British Cartoon Archive, University of Kent, www.cartoons.ac.uk, *r* Topham Picturepoint; **p.69** *t* Solo Syndication/Associated Newspapers Ltd/By permission of Llyfrgell Genedlaethol Cymru/The National Library of Wales, *bl* Evening Standard/Getty Images, *br* Jon/*Daily Mail*, 24 April 1968/British Cartoon Archive, University of Kent, www.cartoons.ac.uk; **p.73** Mac/*Daily Mail*, 16 January 1974/British Cartoon Archive, University of Kent, www.cartoons.ac.uk; **p.74** Giles/Express Syndication/British Cartoon Archive, University of Kent, www.cartoons.ac.uk; **p.76** *tl* Image courtesy of The Advertising Archives, *br* Harold Chapman/Topfoto; **p.78** *l* Imperial War Museum/Knight, Laura Dame RA, *r* Topham Picturepoint; **p.79** Mirrorpix; **p.81** Solo Syndicatin/Associated Newspapers Ltd.; **p.82** *t* The National Archives/HIP/TopFoto, *bl* © TfL from the London Transport Museum collection, *br* Terrence Spencer/Time Life Pictures/Getty Images; **p.84** Reproduced With Permission of Punch Ltd, www.punch.co.uk; **p.87** British Cartoon Archive; **p.88** *l* SSPL via Getty Images, *r* Mary Evans/Classic Stock/Cameriq; **p.91** Image courtesy of The Advertising Archives; **p.92** Trog/*Daily Mail*, 17 May 1968/British Cartoon Archive, University of Kent, www.cartoons.ac.uk; **p.93** Norman Potter/Hulton Archive/Getty Images.

Every effort has been made to trace all copyright holders but if any have been inadvertently overlooked, the Publishers will be pleased to make the necessary arrangements at the first opportunity.

Although every effort has been made to ensure that website addresses are correct at time of going to press, Hodder Education cannot be held responsible for the content of any website mentioned in this book. It is sometimes possible to find a relocated web page by typing in the address of the home page for a website in the URL window of your browser.

Hachette UK's policy is to use papers that are natural, renewable and recyclable products and made from wood grown in sustainable forests. The logging and manufacturing processes are expected to conform to the environmental regulations of the country of origin.

Orders: please contact Bookpoint Ltd, 130 Milton Park, Abingdon, Oxon OX14 4SB. Telephone: +44 (0)1235 827720. Fax: +44 (0)1235 400454. Lines are open 9.00a.m.–5.00p.m., Monday to Saturday, with a 24-hour message answering service. Visit our website at www.hoddereducation.co.uk.

© Rosemary Rees 2010

First published in 2010 by
Hodder Education,
an Hachette UK company
338 Euston Road
London NW1 3BH

Impression number   10 9 8 7 6 5 4 3
Year   2014 2013 2012

Typeset in 11/12pt Bodoni Book by Phoenix Photosetting, Chatham, Kent
Artwork by Barking Dog and Dylan Gibson
Printed and bound in Dubai

A catalogue record for this title is available from the British Library

ISBN 978 0 340 99140 4

Contents

Part 1

Exam advice

Exam advice

Contents

Task

The exam questions will usually focus on just one of the three themes but, because they overlap in time, you will find that your knowledge about one topic may help with your understanding of another.

To help you to see and use these connections, make your own timeline from 1939 to 1975. Make a separate row for each theme: young people, women, immigration. Add events to your timeline as you work through each period.

How to approach the British Depth Study examination

This depth study examines how Britain changed in the years 1939–1975. It focuses on three main themes:

- young people
- women
- immigration.

There is also one focus point about the National Health Service that crosses over these three themes.

The exam will test how well you can understand, evaluate and use sources, but to do that well and to get top marks you will need background knowledge as well. So this book helps you with both aspects of the exam.

- Part 2 (pages 8–73) covers what you need to know about each theme.
- Part 3 (pages 74–93) then gives you practice source investigations.

What types of sources?

In the exam you might come across three types of sources:

- **written sources** such as memoirs, newspaper articles, extracts from history books, interviews
- **pictorial sources** such as posters, cartoons, photographs or paintings
- **statistical sources** such as tables or graphs.

What types of questions?

Every exam is a little different but you will usually meet questions about:

- the **content** of a source – for example 'what can you find out about X from Source Y?'
- the **purpose** or message of a source
- the **reliability** of a source (whether you trust it)
- the **usefulness** of a source for answering a particular question.

You will also have to use:

- **cross-referencing** skills (comparing two or more sources to see if they agree or disagree)
- **evaluation** skills.

And finally you will have to **reach a judgement** taking a whole range of sources into account.

You can see plenty of sample questions in the source investigations on pages 74–93.

HANDY HINTS

1 Read through all the sources before you start writing anything. Make sure you also read
- the background information at the start of the paper, and
- the source captions.

This helps you to understand the sources and answer the questions.

2 All the questions in the exam will be about sources – make sure you use them in all your answers. Never write an answer that makes no use of the sources.

3 Do not write too much in answer to the earlier questions. If a question is worth 6 marks, you will never score more than 6 marks even if you write 19 pages! Answer the question, then move on. Do not try to impress the examiner by writing everything you know about the topic. What they want is an answer to the question.

4 When you are using evidence from sources always make clear to the examiner which source you are using.

5 Always support your answer with examples and explanations.

6 Never try to reach a judgement about a source based simply on what type of source it is. Knowing that a source is an eyewitness account, a photograph or from a memoir does not, in itself, tell you if the source is useful or reliable.
- Do *not* say it is reliable because it is a photograph.
- Do *not* say it is unreliable because it was written much later.
- Do *not* say it is reliable because the person saw what happened.

7 Remember – there are no 'right' answers. The examiner is looking for intelligent answers that are supported by the sources and by your knowledge. Lots of different answers will all be given top marks because they are intelligent answers. Examiners are keen to see original ideas and thinking. So trust your instincts. If you can make a point that is supported by the sources, express it, even if it has not come up in class.

8 Sometimes it will be a good idea to use sources in your answer which are not mentioned in the question. Only do this if it helps you write a better answer. For example, if a question asks you how reliable a source is, one of the other sources in the paper might throw some light on this by contradicting the first source.

9 How do you use your knowledge of the topic? This is a tricky one. The golden rule is only use knowledge if it helps you say something better about the sources mentioned in the question. Your knowledge could be used to help you:
- explain the meaning of a source or the possible purpose of a source
- decide if a source is accurate: check it against what you know about the events
- comment on authorship: you might know something about the author which will help you decide if you trust the source.

10 The final question on the paper will ask you to reach a conclusion about the issue under investigation. Make sure you base your answer on the sources. Remember, the sources will always support two different viewpoints. Make sure you explain how some sources support one viewpoint, then show how other sources support the other viewpoint. Also, say something about how reliable some of the sources are – this will help you reach a conclusion about which viewpoint the sources support the most.

Answering questions about the message or the purpose of a source

One common type of question will ask you about the **message** or the **purpose** of a source. For example:

1 Why was this cartoon published in September 1958?

● **SOURCE A**

A cartoon from the *Daily Mail*, 3 September 1958.

Step 1: Study the source

The first thing to do is look carefully at the cartoon to work out the message. Ask yourself what is happening? Use your knowledge.

Then ask yourself: 'Does the cartoonist approve or disapprove of these teddy boys?' What are the clues that help you decide? The notes in the boxes below will give you some guidance.

> The label 'Notting Hill' and the date shows that this relates to the racial attacks that took place in Notting Hill, London, in September 1958.

> There are three teddy boys slouching and holding knives in a dark alley.

> Even though they are holding knives they don't look threatening. They look ridiculous.

> In a cartoon the words of the caption are nearly always important. This caption is ironic. The teddy boys are claiming to be civilised but their actions show they are not.

Step 2: Answer the question – Why was this cartoon published in September 1958?

The cartoon was clearly published to discredit the people who did the attacks. You now need to use your background knowledge and the details in the source to develop your answer to say why the cartoon was published at that particular time.

Are you surprised by …?

Another way of asking a 'purpose' question is, 'Are you surprised by Source X?' It may not look like it but the question is still asking you to use your background knowledge to explain why the source was published or written at a given time or date. It is your background knowledge that helps you to work out whether a source is typical (so not surprising) or untypical (and therefore surprising).

Tasks

Look at the answer below.
1   What are its strengths?
2   How could it be improved?

This cartoon was published to discredit the people who had attacked immigrants in Notting Hill. In September 1958 there had been three days of fighting and houses were petrol bombed. The attacks were done by teddy boys who had been stirred up by people such as Oswald Mosley. They told them that immigrants were inferior people and should not be allowed to live in Britain. The cartoonist wants us to think that the people who carried out the attack were stupid.

Answering questions about reliability

There will be questions that ask you to comment on the **reliability** of a source or a pair of sources. Sometimes the question will use the word 'reliable'. At other times it will ask you if you **trust** a source or whether you think it is **accurate**. For example:

2 Which source gives more reliable evidence about the causes of racial violence in Notting Hill in 1958, Source A or Source B?

● SOURCE B

Ernest: Most of the white people I talked to seemed annoyed by coloured people keeping brothels in the district. They also agreed that only a tiny minority of people did this but their annoyance seemed quite genuine. They also felt that most of the coloured people in the country were honest people doing an honest job of work but they were very embittered about prostitution in the district.

Reginald: I think that Ernest would agree with me that we have still not really found out what caused this week's riots. Coloured people were very reluctant to come before the camera but all of them I spoke to before the camera or away from it seemed honestly bewildered as to why the riots had happened and also denied that coloured people in the area were any worse than anyone else. What really concerns all of us now is whether these riots are going to reoccur.

> From the BBC television news broadcast about the causes of the Notting Hill riots in 1958. Two reporters went to interview residents after the riots. A black reporter, Ernest Ickle, interviewed the white people; white reporter Reginald Bosanquet interviewed the black people.

How not to answer!

a) Don't make unsupported comments based on who wrote or made the source. For example: 'Source B is more reliable because you can trust the BBC to tell you the truth'; 'Source A is less reliable because cartoons are not meant to be accurate.' These would not get many marks.

b) Don't only use the content of the source. It would be wrong to say 'Source B is more reliable because it mentions some causes of the riots'. A source is not more reliable because it contains more information.

How to answer

Step 1: Examine what the sources say. Look for agreement or disagreement between the sources

Source A blames ignorant and prejudiced teddy boys while Source B mentions some deep grievances about prostitution.

Step 2: Read the caption and consider the provenance and the purpose of the source

Source A was trying to get a point across about the rioters – and particularly about the racist attitudes of the teddy boys – it was not directly addressing the causes of the violence; Source B on the other hand was specifically trying to find out about what caused the riots. Source B is probably more trustworthy – you are told about the methods the interviewers used and who they spoke to. They are also very honest about the fact that they did not really get an answer to their question.

Step 3: Compare what the source is claiming with your own knowledge

When you come to your exam you will know quite a lot about topics like the Notting Hill Riots. This means you can check the sources against what you know. This will tell you that the violence was started by teddy boys, some of whom were stirred up by people such as racist leader Oswald Mosley to attack black people.

There are no right answers to this 'reliability' question – and you don't have to favour one or the other source. You might conclude they are both equally reliable or unreliable. The important thing is that you support your answer with evidence from the source and from your background knowledge.

Answering questions about usefulness

Another common type of exam question asks you about usefulness. Remember, sources can **never** be useful or useless in their own right – it all depends on what they are being used for, so read the whole question: useful for … what? A poster recruiting immigrant workers to come to Britain might be useless for telling you what living or working conditions were actually like for immigrants to Britain but it would be very useful for telling you why immigrant workers were attracted to come to Britain.

3 Read Sources C and D. Which source is more reliable in investigating the experiences of immigrants to Britain?

● **SOURCE C**

Chandra Lal listened to the tales of high wages earned in the factories of Britain. His own uncle regularly sent home money and wrote of life in the industrial Midlands, where the shops were full and nobody went hungry. So, Chandra left his village in India and went to Britain. It was winter when he arrived and the cold wind bit through his thin cotton clothing. Chandra shivered, but found no work because he was not skilled. He went on shivering for four months and at last found a labouring job in Bradford. But Chandra is one of the lucky ones, for there are thousands of other Indians and Pakistanis without work. They think longingly of their villages and the wives and children they left behind.

Extract from a British government leaflet published in India in 1958.

● **SOURCE D**

Our first house was at 65 Westbourne Street. Around 9 or 10 people used to live in the same house. All the white people were really friendly. There was little discrimination but this changed a little when more Asian people started to come over from Africa.

I remember that white people used to live in the same way as us, they used to work hard, wear simple clothes, and they were good people.

Settling in wasn't difficult as we had other family members already here. If they hadn't been here then it may have been more difficult.

I worked in a laundry. I used to get £6 a week. Most people who came in were Gujarati but white people owned it.

The memories of Rambhaben N. Parmar, an Asian woman who came to Leicester from East Africa in 1970 when she was 36. She wrote about her experiences for the web archive 'Moving Here', which gathers the memories of immigrants to Britain.

So how do you approach a 'usefulness' question? It is the same three steps as for reliability.

Step 1: Read or study the content of the source
The exam will not ask trick questions. The sources will always be useful to some degree. You will immediately see that both sources are full of interesting comments on the experiences of the immigrants but just listing their reactions will not earn you top marks.

Step 2: Consider the provenance of the source

One thing to avoid is what the examiners calls 'stock evaluation' (things that could be said about any source), for example, 'Source D is not useful because it is only the view of one person.' That is where your background knowledge helps. You will **know** from your background knowledge how typical a source is.

For Sources C and D the provenance is all important. One of these is a first hand testimony. The other, although it reads like it is a real experience, is actually government propaganda discouraging people from coming to Britain. It reads like a story.

Step 3: Use your background knowledge to put the source and its information in context

Once you have studied this course your background knowledge will tell you why the government wanted to dissuade people from coming to Britain in 1958. You will know that at that time the economy entered a recession and concerns about too much immigration began to surface.

Remember that in a question like this you don't have to choose between the two sources. However in this case, for this question, you might conclude that Source D is very useful but that Source C is fairly useless for understanding the actual experiences. Always make sure you support your answer with details or inferences from the sources.

Cross referencing

Many questions will ask you to use two or more sources. Remember to:

- use all the sources you have been asked to use; don't ignore any of them
- compare the content, detail and provenance to see what they agree or disagree about
- use sentences like these in your answer to help you cross refer:

Both Source A and Source B say that . . .

Source C goes even further than Source D by saying . . .

Source G contradicts Source H by . . .

Answering the big conclusion question

The final question on a source investigation paper is a conclusion question. Our advice on dealing with this kind of question is on page 77.

The changing lives of young people

This book covers a tumultuous period of British history. The six-year trauma of the Second World War was followed by a time of rebuilding and recovery, which led to major social changes. You are going to examine three overlapping themes but first you are going to look at these events through the experiences of young people: what it was like for the wartime generation, the children who endured the hardships of war and its aftermath; and what it was like for the peacetime generation, their children, born into the relative prosperity of the 1950s and 1960s.

What were the experiences of children during the Second World War?

● **SOURCE 1**

This photograph shows children from London sitting outside what had been their home, destroyed in the Blitz. The photo was taken in September 1940.

The Blitz

The Second World War was both a terrifying and exciting time to be a child. From 1940 onwards, the Nazi air force bombed many British cities, London most of all. The aim of the bombing, which was known as the Blitz, was to knock out key industrial centres and also to make ordinary British people suffer so much that they could no longer bear to continue the war.

The Blitz ended in 1941. By that time, over 40,000 British people had been killed, including over 5,000 children, and 1.4 million people had lost their homes.

● **SOURCE 2**

We went up on the moor because we were scared stiff, and we used to snuggle down among the hedges. I'd get my little sister to snuggle into me on one side, my brother on the other side, and the bombs would start dropping. Then you could see the sky starting to light up, and you'd think: 'What part of town is it this time?'

Account by Sid Newham of his experiences of the bombing of Plymouth in 1941.

● SOURCE 3

Dear Rescue Men,
Just a few lines thanking you for what you did for us
on July 14 ... How you helped to get my mother out,
and to get my two brothers which was dead, how you
help me to get to shelter when I hadn't any shoes on
my feet.

Letter from a schoolgirl from Hull, 1943.

● SOURCE 4

Most children were remarkably unaffected by raids.
One Scotswoman recalls that after the heavy blitz on
Clydebank 'my son was thrilled to find bits of shrapnel
in the garden and went round picking them up'. ...
A Kingston woman remembers singing 'in a very
quavery voice' to her small son as they lay beneath her
Morrison [a type of indoor air-raid shelter], until he
complained, 'Mummy, stop singing, I can't hear the
bombs!'

From *How We Lived Then: A History of
Everyday Life During the Second World War*
by Norman Longmate, published in 1971.

The Nazis hoped the Blitz would break the spirit
of the British public. In response, the British
government promoted the idea that the bombing
made the British people all the more united and
more determined to resist Hitler. This idea was
known as the 'Blitz Spirit'.

Although the Blitz did bring people together,
and although people did get more used to living
under the threat of air raids, the 'Blitz Spirit' was
government propaganda: an area where historians
need to treat sources very carefully!

Certainly, from the start of the war adults were
generally very frightened of what was going to
happen. For many children it might have been
the first time they had seen their parents scared,
panicked, crying. A particular fear was that the
Nazis would use gas on civilians. Although this
never happened, gas masks were issued to everyone
and they were a big part of children's lives in the
early years of the war.

● SOURCE 5

Building fell on a group of men and women.
Screams, groans, sudden rush back of people followed
immediately by a rush forward. Women fainted, mass
hysteria, man threw a fit. Men, women and children
crying and sobbing. Frantic parents searching for
their young. Pub nearby full of casualties. Dead and
dying on the pavements. Someone sick.

A Mass Observation report on one of the
first air raids on London in September 1940.
These notes were made by Nina Masel,
who was only 16 when the war began.

A time of fear

Most British children were never bombed so did
not experience the Blitz first-hand, although they
all shared the fear of bombing – no one knew when
or where the next air raid might happen. Likewise,
although Britain was never invaded by the Nazis,
everyone in the UK lived in fear that it would
happen: in the first years of the war it seemed almost
inevitable that it would. These fears had a massive
impact on children at the time, and for many people
their wartime experiences had a big influence on
them for the rest of their lives.

Tasks

1   Study Source 4. Are you surprised that children
    sometimes reacted to air raids in this way?
2   Which of the sources from 1 to 5 do you think
    is most useful for understanding children's
    experiences of the Blitz? Explain why.
3   What impact do you think the war had on
    relationships between children and their
    parents?

Healthy diets

Britain knew from its experiences in the First World War that the Nazis would destroy boats carrying supplies to Britain. Britain imported a lot of food at the start of the Second World War and this needed to change. The more food that could be grown at home, the more space there would be in merchant ships to bring in vital military supplies.

So the government encouraged everyone to grow vegetables. Every scrap of land was planted with crops (even golf courses and playing fields), and everyone tried to make the most of the food they had.

At the same time, some types of food were rationed. The government calculated fair rations for available foods and advised people on how to use them to make healthy meals. What was provided on rations changed from month to month as different foods became available. People had to eat food they wouldn't normally have eaten (like offal or whale meat, for example), there were often shortages of essential foods like sugar, pepper or eggs, and ration amounts were usually pretty small. Not surprisingly, what children most remembered about the war was being hungry!

● **SOURCE 6**

It [the war] makes a lot of difference to me because we have to carry gas masks with us. And the sirens get on my nerves, but the ration of food is terrible. Nearly everything has gone up to an awful lot of money. In one part of the country they have no soap.

Vera, aged 8. Taken from a Mass Observation teaching booklet called 'Children at War'. The booklet was published in 1987 but all the extracts are from interviews with children during the war.

● **SOURCE 7**

	Meat	1 shilling to two shillings and a pennyworth		Tea	2oz–4oz
	Bacon	4oz–8oz		Sugar	8oz–16oz + 2lbs for jam-making
	Cheese	1oz–8oz		Sweets	3oz–4oz (including chocolate)
	Fat	1oz–8oz		Dried milk	1 tin
	Eggs	1–2		Dried eggs	8th of a packet

The weekly ration allowed during the war per adult. Rations of particular foods changed from month to month, depending on the supplies available.

Although children were often hungry, rationing actually made their diet much healthier than it had been before the war. They were eating a lot more vegetables, and not many sweets!

Part-time schools

So, six years of war with only a tiny sweet ration sounds pretty bad, but on the other hand, there was a lot less time at school! A lot of city schools were shut down at the start of the war, when it was expected that most children would be evacuated to the countryside. In fact, only about 50 per cent of town and city children were evacuated, which left large numbers of youngsters, generally from poorer areas, with little to do. At the start of 1940, a third of city children were getting no education at all, and 30 per cent of all children were only going to school for half the day.

As the war progressed, the government realised the impact of the disruption to schooling and reopened some of the schools in the industrial towns. However, they then faced a shortage of teachers: many teachers had been conscripted into the armed forces or other areas of war work. Class sizes increased from an average of around 30 per class to 40, 50 or even 60 children in a class.

When lessons took place, they were often interrupted by air raids. There were very few materials for science experiments or for cookery or sewing classes. Instead of sports, children sometimes did work for farmers. Playground games became dominated by war games (boys often pretended to be Spitfires).

● SOURCE 8

All things considered, and especially in view of the fact that, despite all handicaps and interruptions, the academic and examination results ... have been even better that in pre-1939 sessions, the War has done the boys good. I believe that it has made them face up boldly to genuine facts and problems, it has brought them closer together (even the increase in midday school lunches from 40 to 220 [pupils] is not without significance in this respect), it has emphasised duties rather than privileges, and it has given them a wider outlook on their own future responsibilities. As one boy remarked to me some weeks ago, 'We have finished with "Safety First". We've got to live dangerously ... and don't we know it!'

Report by a headmaster to Mass Observation in March 1943.

● SOURCE 9

There never ought to be wars if we were governed properly. There's always old people in power and the young people are called up and expected to give their lives when they've [the old people] have messed things up. No wonder every generation of young people grow up more restless. I've been to so many different schools since the war's been on that I can't settle down, and then I'm blamed because I don't work well. It's a terrible thing war, such a waste of life and energy, and my opinion is that the country will suffer for years and years.

Interview with Doris, aged 13, by Mass Observation.

Tasks

1 How much of a change do you think rationing and food shortages made to children's lives in the Second World War? Use evidence from Source 6 and Source 7 in your answer.

2 Compare Sources 8 and 9. Which do you think gives the best picture of how the war affected schoolchildren?

Evacuation

● SOURCE 10

This photo shows three evacuees: the photo isn't dated and it isn't clear where it was taken. Notice the luggage labels attached to the boys' coats – evacuees were often labelled in this way. The smaller boxes the children are carrying contain their gas masks.

As soon as the war began in September 1939 the government started evacuating children out of cities into areas less likely to be bombed. This was to try and keep children out of danger, but also so that their mothers would be free to work in industry. The government organised the evacuation of over 800,000 schoolchildren. It was a voluntary scheme – the children were not forced to go.

Evacuated schoolchildren were sent to the countryside, usually to live with complete strangers. Often parents did not even know where their children were going when they waved goodbye to them. As you can imagine, this was often a difficult and confusing time for the children.

Many children from the big cities lived in slum conditions and had never been to the countryside before. And many of the people who lived comfortable lives in the countryside had absolutely no idea that children still lived in such appalling conditions in Britain's big cities.

Many children had good experiences as evacuees, but many others did not. In the very worst cases, children were used as unpaid labour and had to work long hours in hard conditions on farms. There may also have been other kinds of abuse. The experience of evacuation had a lasting effect on most children as they grew up, most in a good way, but in a bad way for others.

● SOURCE 11

The most difficult part of being evacuated is coming home again. It was the worst day of my whole life. When the time came I had completely forgotten my family and London. I was ten years old and suddenly I was to be taken away by this strange lady called Mother, from all these wonderful people I had grown up with and not only from them but the whole village that I knew and loved. I knew every path, track and lane for miles around, every house and cottage, every man, woman and child, every cat, dog, cow and chicken. It was a beautiful world and I had to leave it all behind.

Rene Wingwood, an evacuee from London.

● SOURCE 12

To some unlucky foster-parents it began to seem in those first, disillusioning weeks that life in the back streets of London and other large towns could hardly have changed since Dickensian times. It was, perhaps, the beginning of that great movement of opinion that was to gather momentum throughout the war. At the time, however, the predominant emotion was horror ... A small boy in Oxford astonished the two respectable elderly ladies who had taken him in by helpfully remarking after supper that he would put himself to bed, 'so you two old geezers can get off to the boozer'.

From *How We Lived Then: A History of Everyday Life During the Second World War* by Norman Longmate, published in 1971.

● SOURCE 13

The difficulty seems to be that many of the children have never learned the ordinary decencies of life. What can be done with a child who picks a newspaper and goes into a corner of the drawing room instead of going to the lavatory?... [Many] have never been used to sanitation, and foul the paths and gardens.

One boy said he never went to sleep lying down, he perched himself by the bedpost and went to bed clinging with his head resting on it. There had never been room in the bed at home for him to lie down.

Mrs Rowley, a school teacher in Chepstow, in a report to Mass Observation.

● SOURCE 14

Girl evacuee tries to walk 100 miles

Catherine Brundernell, 12, of Ealing, started to walk the 100 miles home from her billet in the country but was detected at Chippenham, Wilts, after having covered seven miles.

Extract from newspaper story, possibly the *Star*, 1940.

Tasks

1   Using the sources on these pages and your own knowledge, list the reasons why evacuated children might have felt unhappy about their change of life.
2   Now, using the same sources and your own knowledge again, list the reasons why evacuated children might have enjoyed their experiences.
3   Which of the sources on these pages do you think is the most useful in understanding what evacuation must have been like for some inner-city children?
4   What do you think children in the countryside thought of the evacuees? Find sources yourself that give you some information on this.

Key points

What impact did the Second World War have on British children's lives?

- The Blitz was a very frightening experience for many children and parents.
- Evacuation turned the lives of thousands of schoolchildren upside down.
- Better-off families gained direct experience of how poor children lived and they were shocked by what they saw.
- Rationing improved the diets of children but meant they grew up used to shortages.
- People who were children in the Second World War never forgot the huge changes it made to their lives: both good and bad.

In what ways did the Second World War bring about the National Health Service?

Concerns about poverty

Despite the fact that evacuation lasted for only relatively short periods throughout the war, it had a big impact. People living comfortable middle-class lives in the countryside were shocked by the state of children from the big cities. They had not realised before just how bad conditions were for poor people. There was a huge expectation that after the war was over something should be done to help people living in poverty.

● **SOURCE 15**

I never knew such conditions existed, and I feel ashamed of having been so ignorant of my neighbours. For the rest of my life I mean to try and make amends by helping such people to live cleaner, healthier lives.

Conservative politician Neville Chamberlain writing to his sister during the war.

● **SOURCE 16**

The experience of evacuation has shattered complacency and has shown that previous standards of medical inspections for children were too low. Only education, better housing and higher wages will solve the problems of poverty and disease.

From *The Medical Officer*, a journal for health professionals, 1940.

There was also a strong feeling throughout Britain that all the sacrifices of the war years should achieve something more than a return to how things had been in 1939. During the war, the state had taken control of most aspects of people's lives. This meant that after the war, people trusted the state and believed that it could and should do more to create a fairer society.

There was a general election in 1945, the year that the war ended in Europe, and the Labour Party won, beating Winston Churchill's Conservative Party. Although Churchill had led the country through the war, many people wanted change from what had gone before the war. The Labour Party said the government needed to do far more to tackle poverty, illness, poor education and other social problems. And the people agreed.

The Beveridge Report

At the heart of the Labour Party's programme for building a better Britain was a report written in 1942 by a civil servant, Sir William Beveridge. He had been asked to carry out a survey on how existing ways of looking after people (welfare systems) were working and how they could be improved. He identified some major problems.

The Beveridge Report identified 'Five Giants on the Road to Recovery', which appeared in bold, capital letters in the report ('want' means poverty):

WANT, DISEASE, IGNORANCE, SQUALOR and **IDLENESS**.

Beveridge proposed to defeat these giants through full employment (all adults having a job) and a comprehensive welfare system, including a free National Health Service and child allowances (see Source 17).

● SOURCE 17

Family allowances

Cost met by the government

Free healthcare

Flat rate benefits for the unemployed and the sick

National Insurance covering everyone from the cradle to the grave

A summary of Beveridge's proposals.

What was really different about Beveridge's ideas was that everyone should pay the same towards the welfare state so that everyone could get the same support back from it. This was a big change from previous schemes for helping poorer people, which were often based on the idea that people could get money once they'd passed certain tests – called means-testing.

Reactions to the Beveridge Report

Although some politicians within the wartime government thought the report was far too ambitious, there was a lot of public interest in the report and a huge level of support for its suggestions. When Churchill said that people would have to wait until after the war and see what money the country had left to pay for such a programme, people could see the sense of that. But in 1945 the country wanted the government to take action quickly and the Labour Party were the ones who promised to do what Beveridge had suggested if they were elected.

● SOURCE 18

This cartoon was published in the *Daily Mail* in February 1943. The man about to light the fuse is Sir William Beveridge.

Tasks

1   What evidence can you find from the sources here and on pages 12–13 to suggest that the condition of some evacuees opened people's eyes to how some children were living in British cities?
2   The cartoon in Source 18 shows Beveridge looking to Churchill for permission to light the fuse to his barrel of dynamite. What is the message of this cartoon? Use the source and your knowledge to explain your answer.
3   Using the sources and your own knowledge, explain how the Second World War made people more confident that the state could organise social support in Britain.

The creation and impact of the National Health Service

When the Labour Party won its great victory in 1945, the new government set out to put Beveridge's ideas into practice – and to go still further. It introduced a whole range of far-reaching measures.

Date	Measure	Provision
1945	Family Allowances Act	Allowance of five shillings per week per child in any family.
1946	National Insurance Act	Benefits for any worker who was unemployed, injured or sick.
1946	National Health Service Act	The NHS was set up in 1948 and gave free healthcare to all.
1947	Town and Country Planning Act and New Towns Act	Clearance of slums and bomb-damaged housing and relocation of many of the poorest in Britain's cities to new towns.
1948	Children's Act	Local authorities required to set up services for the protection of children.
1949	Housing Act	A massive programme of building new housing to meet the latest specifications.

The National Health Service was a central part of this programme and its creation had a huge and long-lasting impact on people's lives. It wasn't the case that there had been no healthcare for poorer families before the war: there had been many insurance schemes that gave them access to medical help. However, richer people could always get much better treatment than the poor. Because the state was providing the National Health Service, it meant that everyone had access to the same level of healthcare, paid for by everyone out of taxation.

Before the war:

- workers usually had free access to a doctor (GP), but their families didn't
- sometimes families paid a small amount each month into a local insurance scheme so they could afford to see a doctor if they needed it
- it was quite common for doctors to charge rich patients a bit more so they could afford to charge poorer patients less
- there was a complex patchwork of hospitals: municipal hospitals run by local councils, charity hospitals, teaching hospitals – each hospital was different from the next.

After 1948:

- the state paid doctors to treat everyone free of charge: doctors could top up this salary by charging fees to private patients
- hospitals came under state control so they could treat everyone equally, free of charge. The state paid hospital consultants, but they could also see private patients for a fee.

● **SOURCE 19**

The same services were available the day after the creation of the NHS as the day before, no new hospitals were built nor hundreds of new doctors employed. But poor people who often previously went without medical treatment now had access to services, instead of relying instead on dubious and sometimes dangerous home remedies or the charity of doctors who gave their services free to their poorest patients.

'National Health Service History' by Geoffrey Rivett, www.nhshistory.net/shorthistory.htm

● SOURCE 20

There are many moving accounts of the queues of unwell and impoverished people surging forward for treatment in the early days of the NHS, arriving in hospitals and doctors' waiting rooms for the first time not as beggars but as citizens with a sense of right.

From *A History of Modern Britain* by Andrew Marr, published in 2007.

● SOURCE 21

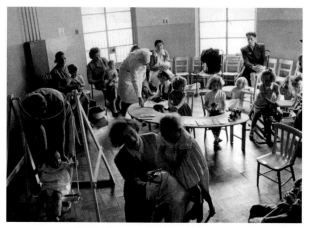

This picture is from July 1948 and shows a nurse with mothers and children at a clinic for regular health checks. This service was provided free on the National Health Service.

● SOURCE 22

I was for the change [to the NHS] because I had done my training in Glasgow where there were very poor people, and mothers who had no antenatal care [care before giving birth]. There weren't enough beds in the hospital, so most births were at home. Some of these women were afraid of the hospital, very much afraid. Often, the maternity deaths were in hospital, because the only people who came in were those who had complications, and that contributed to the fear of hospitals.

Margaret Grieve: in 1948 she was a newly-qualified midwife working in a council-run maternity hospital in Dumfries. Interview with Margaret Grieve in 'The birth of the NHS' by Andy McSmith, *The Independent*, 28 June 2008.

● SOURCE 23

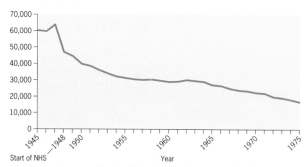

Infant mortality in Britain in the twentieth century.

Tasks

1 What are the strengths and limitations of Source 23 for explaining the impact that the creation of the NHS had on children's health?
2 How useful is Source 22 in explaining how the NHS improved care for new mothers and their babies?
3 To what extent was the NHS something completely new? Which sources could you use to identify elements of continuity rather than change?

Key points

What was the impact of the National Health Service on people's lives?

- The experiences of the war meant that by 1948 most British people were prepared for the state to organise a National Health Service, paid for by everybody.
- Before the NHS, poorer people could not always afford doctors' fees. After the NHS, everyone had access to a good standard of healthcare.
- The NHS had a big impact on the lives of women, for example women got much better care during childbirth.
- With the NHS, parents could take children to the doctor, dentist or optician without worrying about how they would afford the cost of treatment.
- With the NHS, hospitals were run centrally by the state so that people would get the same standard of care where they lived in the country and regardless of whether they were poor or better off.

What was it like growing up in the 1950s?

The 1950s are often seen as a 'transitional' decade in British history: caught halfway between the war years of the 1940s and the great social changes of the 1960s. Britain's economy was ruined by the Second World War and rationing had to continue into the 1950s. Tea was rationed until 1952, sugar and eggs until 1953 and cheese and meat stayed rationed until 1954. Bread did not start to be rationed until *after* the war had ended. Families who had enough money could buy difficult-to-find things through the illegal 'black market'.

Adults found the continuing tough times difficult to deal with – after all, weren't things supposed to get better once the war had finished? But most people who were children in the 1950s remember it as being a wonderful time to grow up. These children generally had no memory of families being able to buy whatever food they wanted. And when people look back on their 1950s childhoods now, many stress the freedom that they had in comparison to the lives of children today.

Teenagers

In the early 1950s there wasn't anything like the teenage culture of today. Young people didn't have a separate sort of culture from adults: they wore the same sorts of clothes as their parents and had the same pastimes as their parents. Families ate together, watched TV together (there was only one channel to watch anyway) and listened to the radio together. They often went to the same schools their parents had done, and might well go on to work for the same companies as their parents did.

● SOURCE 24

I started school in 1951 and compared with what kids have today we had very little. We didn't have a television, although I knew some families that did. It was a real badge of honour to have a television mast on your roof. We had enormous freedom: you could just say 'I'm off for a cycle ride' and off you'd go. It was an age of great innocence. I suppose, looking back on it, our demands were small but then we didn't know any different. The great age of the teenager hadn't really come in: we thought of ourselves as young and as not knowing as much as grownups – and they encouraged us in this view! As far as I know there weren't teenage magazines, although we did have pin ups and fantasies – mine was the actor Laurence Olivier and my friend Mary Taylor's was Peter May the cricketer: grown-up idols. We modelled ourselves on grown-up film stars. There was an advert that said 'nine out of ten films stars use Lux soap'. I don't remember any young teenage pin-ups until Tommy Steele and Cliff Richard at the end of the 1950s.

Margaret Bircher, born in 1939.

Through the 1950s, as Britain's economy improved, there weren't enough people for all the jobs on offer. Anyone who was fit for a job could get one; and employers had to push up wages to keep their staff from leaving and getting another job, or to attract the best people to new jobs. So in a short time families went from not having enough money (not that there was much to buy legally anyway), to there being both plenty of things to buy and enough money to spend on them.

These economic changes also meant the start of some important changes for teenagers:

- it was easy to get a job when you left school
- trade unions had made sure that most jobs had reasonable working hours. Most people worked just five days a week, instead of the long hours and six-day weeks of earlier decades
- fathers usually earned enough money to keep the household, so teenagers could keep a lot of the money they earned for themselves.

All this meant that teenagers could start to create a separate sort of identity from their parents. Teenagers had money, and companies started targeting them as consumers. Some teenagers started to dress differently, to listen to different music, to watch films that their parents might not approve of, to spend more time with other teenagers than with their families. A lot of the new trends came from America. It was easy for these trends to come to the UK because of the common language of English. The war had begun this process: thousands of American soldiers had been stationed in Britain during the war and had introduced local people to American fashion and youth culture; and the advent of television in the 1950s continued it.

● **SOURCE 25**

Two British teenagers in 1959.

● **SOURCE 26**

Police were called to cinemas in London and Liverpool last night to deal with disturbances among youthful audiences at showings of the film Rock Around the Clock ... *Youths threw lighted cigarettes from the circle onto people sitting in the stalls. Others sprayed parts of the cinema with water from hose pipes. Girls in the audience struggled to get outside.*

Report from *The Times* newspaper, 11 September 1956. The film *Rock Around the Clock* was banned by some UK councils following other disturbances like those described here.

© *The Times* and 11.09.1956/nisyndication.com

Tasks

1   Write a Facebook-style page for a 13-year-old in the early 1950s, describing their lifestyle, favourite foods and what they like to do with their spare time. Then update it for the same teenager when they are 17, in the late 1950s. Use the sources, any further research and your own imagination!
2   Do you think that all teenagers in the later 1950s dressed like the two in Source 25? To what extent is this picture a reliable representation of what it was like to grow up in the 1950s?

Key points

What was it like growing up in the 1950s?

- The early years of the 1950s were a struggle: there was bomb damage everywhere, shortages of everything and rationing continued.
- The later years of the 1950s saw full employment and prosperity.
- Early in the 1950s teenagers acted like their parents: there wasn't really a separate 'youth culture'.
- However, as teens got money of their own and more free time they started to create a separate identity. Sometimes this identity clashed with the older generation.

Why were there changes in the lives of teenagers in the 1960s?

Although the 1960s did bring in big changes in the ways teenagers lived their lives, in some ways the 1960s continued trends that had started in the later 1950s and built on them, making them stronger and more dramatic. In other ways, new trends did emerge in the 1960s, particularly as a result of teenagers becoming more political.

There were many reasons for the changes, including:

- Science and technology: for example, the development of the oral contraceptive pill, which started to become available in the UK in 1960 (see page 43); new fabrics made new fashions possible; space travel opened up new ways of thinking about the future.
- Economic factors: teenagers continued to have plenty of money to spend and companies marketed products specifically for them.

- Political factors: teenagers were increasingly influenced by radical politics, like feminism (see pages 42–45), environmentalism, communism, pacifism.
- Cultural factors: the sixties were a time of great cultural experimentation, especially in music, lifestyle and fashion; Britain's cities were also increasingly multicultural.
- Individuals: some key individuals set the fashions of the 1960s – musicians, authors, poets, playwrights, designers, etc.

However, although the 1960s did bring about many changes in the lives of teenagers, remember that the decade was not all about change. For most teenagers these changes didn't really make much of an impact on their lives.

Tasks

1   Study the sources opposite, which are all related to advertising aimed at young people in the 1960s. Decide which sources best match the following advertising messages:
    - Designed for young men
    - Designed for young women
    - About freedom
    - About sexuality
    - About celebrity
    - About innocent fun
    - About glamorous lifestyles
    - Contains links to political themes
    - Unlikely to appeal to older people
2   Now link each source to a reason for change in teenagers' lives in the 1960s: for example for Source 27, **economic changes** meant teenagers had more money to spend on items such as scooters; for Source 28, **technological changes** meant record players became more portable.
3   Sources 27 and 30 are adverts. Are adverts automatically unreliable sources? Explain your answer.

Key points

Why were there changes in the lives of teenagers in the 1960s?

- In some ways the 1960s just continued and intensified the trends of the 1950s: teens had money and free time to do their own thing.
- In other ways the 1960s saw new changes in the lives of teenagers. The biggest were related to direct political challenges to authority.
- The 1960s also saw big social changes generally: attitudes to sex and drugs were not as strict and this had an impact on young people's lives.

● **SOURCE 27**

A 1960s advert for a Lambretta scooter. What does the line 'Let yourself go on a Lambretta' mean? Is there more than one meaning?

● **SOURCE 28**

This is the cover of an annual for teenage girls from 1968.

● **SOURCE 29**

A magazine cover from 1968. The pictures are all of UK and US pop stars. The magazine was named after a character in the TV show *Thunderbirds*.

● **SOURCE 30**

This advert for underwear in the 1960s includes the line: 'give your tummy a thrilling taste of freedom' (by wearing a Berlei girdle).

● **SOURCE 31**

This music magazine cover features the Rolling Stones in their early days, 1963.

● **SOURCE 32**

This girls' magazine is from 1967. In the tag-line 'Young, gay and get-ahead', the word 'gay' means carefree, happy.

How did teenagers and students behave in the 1960s and early 1970s?

Teenagers as consumers: music and fashion

In the early 1960s the five million teenagers in the UK spent about £800 million per year on themselves – mainly on clothes, cosmetics and entertainment. This was a big market and companies targeted teenagers with products specifically designed for them: this was the first time this had happened in the UK. At the same time, teenagers responded also to individuals doing their own thing, especially with music and fashion. There was a move away from the 'manufactured' pop groups of the 1950s in favour of groups that played songs they wrote themselves, like the Beatles.

● SOURCE 33

Teenage affluence was undoubtedly the single biggest factor in explaining the spectacular development of popular music between the mid-fifties and the early sixties ... In 1955 British listeners bought just over 4 million 45-rpm singles a year; by 1960, they were buying 52 million; and by 1963, 61 million. Record companies and retailers recognised that they would make more money if they emphasised styles that appealed to the young, rather than the romantic ballads and big-band music that appealed to their parents.

From *White Heat: A History of Britain in the Swinging Sixties* by Dominic Sandbrook, published in 2006.

● SOURCE 34

Person A
I had an almost total obsession with pop music. I would play records all the time. You'd go and buy a record – a little 45 rpm, maybe one a fortnight – and you'd just play it over and over.

Person B
I went to the Beatles concert at the Wigan Ritz with Gene Pitney and Mary Wells also on the bill. I wore a pencil-slim skirt and I spent the whole time screaming. I have no idea what they sang, but I remember the camaraderie of everyone there. We were all so happy to be there, part of a huge party.

Person C
The sixties began for me when I discovered the Rolling Stones. I hated the teachers at school. I hated authority, so when the Rolling Stones appeared on the scene I was immediately attracted ...

Three separate people remember being a teenager in the 1960s, quoted in *Changing Times: Being Young in Britain in the '60s* by Alison Pressley, published in 2000.

● SOURCE 35

Person A
The music was great. I can remember going with my brother Mike and all his friends to see Pink Floyd at Knebworth Festival ... I can remember returning with Mike, and us both agreeing that, while we didn't believe in God, the nearest thing to God on this earth was definitely Pink Floyd. They understood us.

Person B
I liked David Cassidy and Donny Osmond and David Essex. A friend of ours in class liked the Bay City Rollers and we looked down on her, we thought that was too awful.

Person C
When glam rock came in, you insisted on watching Top of the Pops on Thursday night mainly to enrage your father, because there'd be men with makeup on. If you got your dad and your granddad in the same room you got double score. They couldn't understand what was going on at all.

Three separate people remember being a teenager in the early 1970s, quoted in *The Seventies: Good Times, Bad Taste* by Alison Pressley, published in 2002.

● SOURCE 36

This photo from 1967 shows shoppers examining the racks of clothes outside the boutique called 'I Was Lord Kitchener's Valet' on Portobello Road, London.

● SOURCE 37

A woman shopping in the trendy clothes shop 'Top Gear' on the King's Road in Chelsea in 1965.

Tasks

1   Sort the six different quotes in Sources 34 and 35 into the following two categories about why music mattered so much to young people in the 1960s and early 1970s:
   • related to identity – the music helps young people understand who they are and how they feel
   • related to differences – the music helps young people sort out who is like them and who they are not like.

2   Source 33 puts forward the hypothesis that record companies continued to deliberately 'design' bands for the teenage and student market in the 1960s and early 1970s. To what extent do the other sources here support that view?

3   Sources 36 and 37 both show very fashionable shops in 1960s London. What impressions do these photos give you about the sort of shops these were, and the sorts of people who might go into them?

4   Source 36 shows a group of young men dressed up in similar military uniform-style clothes. What influences do you think might have convinced them this was a cool thing to do?

5   Source 37 shows a young woman scrutinising Top Gear's jackets. Outside the shop window an older woman, dressed in a 1950s style, is peering in. Assuming that the photographer (called David Cairns) deliberately captured this moment, what message do you think he was trying to convey?

Rebellion and the development of a youth culture

There's a famous line in the 1953 film, *The Wild One*, when Marlon Brando's character, Johnny, is asked 'What are you rebelling against?' Johnny replies 'Watcha got?' The character of Johnny set the mould for Hollywood teenage rebels, angry at everything. And those films connected with teenagers in Britain too, making rebellion part of a distinct youth culture in the 1950s and 1960s.

Adolescents have always rebelled against their parents, but in the 1960s teens found specific ways to channel their feelings. Here are a few ideas about what teens might have been rebelling against:

- the 1950s: ideas about duty, respectability, obeying orders, doing what other people did, buttoned-up (and often hypocritical) attitudes to sex and drugs
- the war generation: teens in the 1960s had parents who had fought and suffered in the war – a hard act to follow. Imagine always being told, 'I didn't fight Hitler so you could ...'
- boredom: teens in the 1960s had money and leisure time but not always anything to do with it
- political manipulation and deceit: the 1960s saw the first real challenges to the belief that politicians were trustworthy and always did the best for the country
- social changes: for example, immigration (see pages 48–73) and changes in women's role in society (see pages 30–47)
- disappointment or frustration that Britain was not living up to their hopes or expectations
- each other: teen culture immediately fragmented into different, competing groups, such as the Mods and the rockers.

● SOURCE 38

Inspector G. Brown said that the five youths, in motor cycling clothes, were walking peacefully along the sea wall, when a gang of Mods 'descended on them like a pack of vultures, and started to put the boot in'. He said that he saw Mr Taylor [aged 17] leading the gang, and Mr Smith [aged 18] kicking at the youths.

From *The Times* newspaper, 30 August 1967.
© *The Times* and 30.08.1967/nisyndication.com

● SOURCE 39

As a sixteen-year-old, my parents forbade me to go out alone with a boy, to ride on the back of a motor scooter, to drink, to go to a club where the Rolling Stones played ... So one night I deliberately broke every one of their norms [rules of behaviour]. I went on the back of my boyfriend's scooter to the club, listened to the Stones and got drunk, and [had sex] in his house before going home. It wasn't just adolescent rebellion against being controlled, though that was part of it. There was something keener, fresher in the air. A sense that we were going to do things our way, and that there were a lot of us who rejected not just our individual parents but what their values represented socially.

Recollections of interviewee Elisabeth Tailor about her life as a teenager in the 1960s, quoted in 'Student Revolution in 1960s Britain: Myth or Reality?', by Patrick H. J. Smith, 2007 (www.patricksmith.org.uk).

● **SOURCE 40**

This is a scene from an anti-Vietnam war demonstration in June 1966 in Grosvenor Square, London.

● **SOURCE 41**

I remember the Cuban Missile Crisis of 1962 vividly, genuinely thinking that the world was going to end. Every night the news would come on with a map, showing how far the Russian ships had got towards the American blockade. You could predict the number of days it would take them to reach it. I remember thinking, I ought to do things now, because if the world is blown up I won't get the chance.

Quoted in *Changing Times: Being Young in Britain in the '60s* by Alison Pressley, published in 2000.

There were many ways in which young people in the 1960s were challenging authority, trying to get their voices heard, living their lives according to new ways of thinking. Youth culture defined itself as much by what it was against as what it was for – a counterculture.

However, it is important, too, to keep rebellion against the older generation in context. Most teenagers did not 'drop out' of society. Only a tiny minority of teenagers fought each other on the beaches of the southern coast. Student protests in Britain were extremely law-abiding affairs when compared with the unrest in France and the USA in the late 1960s and 1970s. Perhaps what had changed most was not teenagers, but the way the media reacted to them.

Task

Study the sources on pages 24 and 25. What can each source tell us about why students in the 1960s and early 1970s were rebelling against authority?

The reactions of the authorities to changes in teenage and student behaviour

Who were 'the authorities'? This is a broad term that can cover everyone from the government down to parents: in the sixties and seventies young people often referred to 'the Man' – those who controlled power in society. The generation making up the authorities was the one that had fought in the Second World War, who had sacrificed and suffered so much to ensure their children grew up in a free society rather than a fascist dictatorship. So it is perhaps not surprising that the general reaction to the teenage counterculture was not always that positive!

There are lots of sources describing the ways the authorities reacted to the great changes in youth behaviour, fashion, music and politics in the 1960s and early 1970s. As you can imagine, there were lots of newspaper articles, debates in parliament, research projects, academic papers, memoirs and letters written about teenage behaviour, as well as other types of sources. For these two pages, however, we are going to focus on political cartoons. You will need to know how to use a wide range of sources for this topic in your exam, but cartoons are a good source of information on reactions and they often require the trickiest source analysis skills, which is why we will practise using them here.

● **SOURCE 42**

The published caption for this 1960 cartoon from the *Daily Express* reads: 'The poor darling! The medicine we've been giving him is much too nasty!' As well as a gun, the teenager is carrying a flick knife and wearing 'winkle picker' shoes.

Tasks

1 Look at Source 42. Describe what the teenage character is wearing and holding, and what message these carry for the cartoon's audience. Make sure you always link a description with a significance. For example, the character is wearing a leather jacket and has a quiff hairstyle: this shows he is a 'rocker', a type of teenager linked by the authorities to violent clashes with Mods.

2 What message does Source 42 give about why teenagers have turned out so badly, such a contrast from the 'bonny child' on the medicine bottle?

3 The people shown holding the medicine bottle in Source 42 are well-meaning health professionals and educators who have concocted this 'modern mixture' for bringing up children. Using this information, explain the purpose of this cartoon. Who does the cartoonist blame for the problems of modern youth and why does he say things have gone wrong?

● SOURCE 43

This cartoon is titled 'Looking for trouble'. A policeman is looking round a corner at teenager rockers, ignoring all the sexual scandals, pornography, indecent behaviour and gambling with which adult society is obsessed. It was published in the *Daily Mail* in April 1964.

● SOURCE 44

'Yes, a lovely Easter, thanks. One protest march, two demonstrations, and three super outbreaks of violence.'

A cartoon from the *Daily Mail*, August 1968. Cartoonists often enjoyed contrasting peace protestors with violent demonstrations.

Tasks

4 Source 43 suggests that much of the way the authorities reacted to changes in teenage and student behaviour was deeply hypocritical. The authorities were so critical about young people's attitudes to sex, drugs, violence and politics, when there were just as many problems in the rest of society. Study the cartoon carefully and list the details included to get its message across.

5 What message does Source 44 give about how the authorities might have viewed student protest? Explain how the cartoonist gets this message across.

Key points

How did teenagers and students behave in the 1960s and early 1970s?

- Big companies targeted teens with products designed for them – this trend had started in the 1950s.
- However, young people making their own music or fashion were also hugely popular and respected.
- Teens and students identified strongly with the music, fashion and lifestyles that were created for them and by them.
- Some young people rejected what older people said about how they should behave. There was a clash between the generations.

How far did the lives of all teenagers change in the 1960s and early 1970s?

A danger for historians is that the sixties seem so important to us today that we exaggerate the impact of changes in that period. Was there a revolution in the 1960s that affected everyone in society? Or were these changes slower to develop? Were they even long-term trends that had a starting point way before the 1960s?

For example, the common view of the 1960s is that young people had more sex, with more people, earlier. The contraceptive pill is usually given as a major reason for this change: teenage girls did not need to worry so much about getting pregnant.

There certainly were changes in sexual behaviour in the 1960s, but to what extent did these changes affect all teenagers?

● **SOURCE 45**

Teenagers in the sixties were the first generation since the war to decide that the mysteries of sex should be explored and discoveries made for the sheer fun of it. People had sex at the slightest excuse after meeting for only ten minutes. Sexual partners were snapped up and discarded without ceremony, provided that they had the newly available contraceptive pill in their pocket or handbag.

An extract from *The Swinging Sixties* by Brian Masters, published in 1985.

● **SOURCE 46**

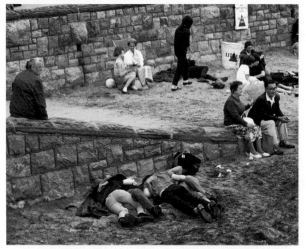

This photo of a 1964 beach scene includes young couples canoodling (in the foreground). Other beach users are not obviously objecting – at least, not at the point that the photo was taken.

● **SOURCE 47**

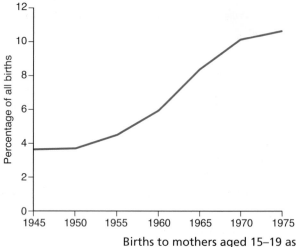

Births to mothers aged 15–19 as percentage of all births, 1945–1975.

● SOURCE 48

[T]he belief that sexual activity among the unmarried young is more common than it used to be is based on impressions, because we have little detailed information about the past. Some believe that this behaviour only seems more common because it is now more obvious and more freely admitted.

'Sexual Promiscuity Among Students',
British Medical Journal, 25 March 1967.

● SOURCE 49

Throughout the investigation modern methods of random sampling and statistical analysis were applied and special care has been taken to avoid sources of potential error in earlier studies, in which groups such as students have been used as subjects because they were readily available, or older people have been asked to remember the sexual adventures of their youth. Particular care was taken to keep down the number of refusals to co-operate, which was in fact under 15%.

From the present investigation it appeared that 11% of 478 boys aged 15 to 17 and 6% of 475 girls of the same age had had sexual intercourse at least once. The same admission was made by 30% of 456 older boys aged 17 to 19 and by 16% of 464 girls of the same age ...

From 'Sexual Behaviour of Young People' – a review of *The Sexual Behaviour of Young People* by Michael Schofield, 1965, in the *British Medical Journal*, 31 July 1965.

Tasks

1 Evaluate how reliable each source is as evidence of trends in young people's sexual behaviour. Which of these sources do you think is the most and least reliable, and why?

2 Source 49 includes information on how its data were collected. It identifies some problems with earlier studies:
   • using students as readily-available subjects
   • asking older people to remember sexual experiences when they were young
   • only including young people who are immediately ready to talk about sexual experiences.
   Why would each of these be a problem for source reliability?

3 'Source 47 is the most useful source for this enquiry because its data clearly show a sharp rise in young people having sex in the 1960s.' To what extent would you agree with this statement? (Consider whether births are a reliable indicator of all sexual activity.)

4 How far do the sources on these pages support the view that the sex lives of most teenagers changed dramatically from the 1950s to the 1960s?

Key points

How far did the lives of all teenagers change in the 1960s and early 1970s?

• The sixties have become famous for massive social changes: particularly in relation to moral standards – sex, drugs, hippy lifestyles, etc.
• However, while teenagers did all have access to information on new ways of thinking and behaving, for most teens life went on much as before.
• For the historian, changes in sexual behaviour are very difficult to measure because this is the most private area of people's lives.

The changing role of women, 1939–1975

In 1973 Margaret Thatcher, who was then Education Secretary, said 'I don't think there will be a woman Prime Minister in my lifetime.' She of course went on to become the first woman Prime Minister of Britain just six years later. It was a fitting conclusion to 30 years of great change in the role of women. This chapter investigates the main changes and the reasons for them.

What impact did the Second World War have on women in the years to 1951?

What did you do in the war, Mummy?

Once war was declared, women flooded into the workplace. They were recruited by the Ministry of Labour and the National Service to fill the gaps left by men entering the armed services. Conscription for men had been introduced from the very start of the war in 1939 and, aware of the crucial part women had played in the previous world war, the government swung into immediate action. The economy of the country had to be kept going while men were away fighting. It had to be geared up to support an army, navy and air force that were at war, and it had to support a civilian population, too.

What work was the government expecting women to do?

Serving in the armed forces

Almost one million women worked in the armed forces. Many women, once they had joined up, found themselves doing exactly the same tasks as they would have done in peacetime: cooking and serving meals, and general clerical work. However, for some there was more exciting, interesting and adventurous work. In the Women's Auxiliary Air Force (WAAF) there were women who worked as radio operators and signallers; they operated barrage balloons and flew aircraft from factories where they were made to the airfields that needed them. In the Women's Royal Naval Service (WRNS) they took weather readings and made forecasts, tested torpedoes and depth charges, repairing them if necessary. In the Auxiliary Territorial Service (ATS) women worked as drivers of jeeps, lorries and cars, maintaining them as well as driving senior officers around. They also rode motorbikes as dispatch-riders, and worked as draughtswomen, accurately mapping the countryside. No woman was sent to a combat zone and so did not have to kill.

● **SOURCE 1**

These posters were produced by the government during the Second World War.

Tasks

Look at Source 1.

1. How is the government trying to persuade women to go out to work?
2. Not every poster in the source is trying to encourage women to go out to work. One is trying to persuade women to do something else. What is that, and why?
3. What different techniques are the government using in these posters?
4. Which poster do you think is the most persuasive? Why?

Secrets and spies

The most difficult service to get into was the Special Operations Executive (SOE) because you had to be specially invited to join. The SOE was set up to work with the French Resistance to create havoc behind enemy lines by doing things such as blowing up bridges, cutting telephone lines and sabotaging railway signals. SOE members often also worked as couriers and wireless operators sending crucial information back to Britain. The women, who had to be expert linguists, were given new identities and parachuted behind enemy lines. Altogether, about 3,000 women were recruited by the SOE, though they didn't all work abroad. Those who stayed in Britain did important work behind the scenes, for example, de-coding messages, creating fake documents and disguises, and arranging secret journeys.

Working on the land

At the start of the war the government asked Lady Reading (a society lady known for her energy and determination to get things done) to begin the organisation of a Women's Land Army. Unfortunately, she didn't see the need to talk to, or even work with, the agricultural trade unions. This meant that farmers were initially reluctant to employ women workers, or land girls, so of the 17,000 volunteers who enrolled at the start of the war, only 5,000 found places on farms. However, by 1943 the situation had reversed: thousands of women were working the land and there were not enough recruits to go round. Land girls did every kind of farm work: for example, tractor driving, ploughing, milking, fruit spraying and tree felling.

Working in industry

The government set up training schemes for women workers in a large range of different skills, from oxy-acetylene welding to motor mechanics, and these women became skilled operatives in a huge number of factories and workshops. Women worked in the construction industry, in the chemical industry and in the transport industry. Women could be found plumbing, shovelling coal, operating cranes, delivering letters, driving buses and in a thousand and one other jobs that kept the economy going.

Trouble ahead?

There was trouble ahead, however. As well as working, most women had families to look after, too. This had not been the case when men had been the main workers in industry – very few of them had to go home to wash nappies, mend clothes and cook a meal! Women began demanding help with their childcare, and were angry that nurseries were not readily available for all working mothers. They began asking, too, why they were not getting paid the same as men for doing the same work.

● **SOURCE 2**

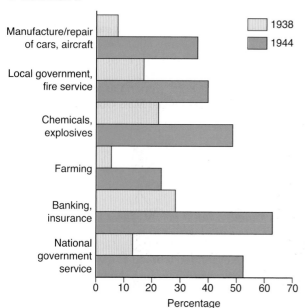

The percentage of women employees working in various industries in 1938 and in 1944.

Tasks

5 Look at Source 2. How useful would this source be to a historian trying to find out about the success of women's war work?

6 Read the information about the war work done by women. Write a paragraph explaining whether or not you think it likely that they would want to stop work and return to being purely wives and mothers.

1945: back to normal?

On 7 May 1945, German radio broadcast that their General Alfred Jodl would sign the official surrender of Nazi Germany the following day. Winston Churchill, the British Prime Minister, immediately announced that 8 May 1945 would be celebrated as VE (Victory in Europe) Day. The war was over – in Europe, at least. The Second World War did not finally end until Japan surrendered on 15 August 1945 – VJ Day.

Housewife or employee?

Many women who had worked either full- or part-time during the war years wanted to continue working and combine their work with family life. However, the government, which had been desperate to recruit women workers to keep the economy going during the dark days of the war, expected them to return to their homes now that the war was over and the men were back. Most employers and many men agreed. Not all women were so certain, however.

● SOURCE 3

I think that marriage is a full-time career, though not as exciting as one outside the home, perhaps; and a woman cannot give of her best to two careers. On the whole, I think that married women will be only too glad to make their home the centre of their life.

Single woman, companion and home help, aged 56, Bristol, interviewed by Mass Observation in 1944.

● SOURCE 4

Where women have had careers, and where they are more suited to continue working than to spend time housekeeping and baby-minding, I think they should work. It is far better for a woman to continue with the job for which she is suited, and to pay the right kind of person to look after her home and children, than to become a drudge herself, if housework is drudgery to her. But I think a married woman should work no more than 40 hours a week, and she should always consider her family before her job. I am hoping for a development of Day Nurseries, all jobs open to married women and maternity grants.

Married woman, no children, aged 28, working as an aerodynamicist in Winchester, Hampshire, interviewed Mass Observation in 1944.

● SOURCE 5

[In the spring of 1945] there were about twelve women welders in the shipyard. We were sent for one morning and the personnel officer sat there at his desk. He lifted his head and he said one word – 'redundant'. That was a new word to our vocabulary. We really didn't know exactly what it meant. There was no reason given. There was no explanation. There was plenty of work in the yard.

Before the war Bella Keyzer had worked as a weaver in Dundee. Then she was sent by the government into shipbuilding where she was trained as a welder. She enjoyed the work but was forced to give it up in 1945. Here she recounts how her job came to an end.

● SOURCE 6

I am just beginning to appreciate some of the advantages that help to off-set the financial loss brought about by Marjorie's change over from office work to house-wifery. I am able to have all my meals at home instead of going up to Mother's for breakfast and round to the British Restaurant for lunch, as well as no longer having to do any housework, such as washing, wiping-up, sweeping, dusting, fire-lighting etc etc. One certainly has a more comfortable time of it with a bustling wife around the house.

Anthony Heap, a middle-aged local government officer living in London, clearly found his life more comfortable when his wife Marjorie became a full-time housewife again. We don't know what Marjorie thought!

● SOURCE 7

Men hate their girls going out to work and impairing their own dignity as head of the house.

A trade union leader in the north-east of England explains to the writer James Lansdale Hodson why men prefer women to stay at home.

● SOURCE 8

Your "after-the-war" dream . . .

is coming true ... war duties ended ... Dad finished with night shifts ... family reunions. Peacetime interests and new cares.
Now yours will be the responsibility of looking after the family's health. Wartime experience has shown you the value of 'Milk of Magnesia', so you won't forget to keep this always in the medicine cabinet as a stand-by against the minor upsets of the system.

'MILK OF MAGNESIA'

'Milk of Magnesia' is the trade mark of Phillips' preparation of magnesia

An advertisement for Milk of Magnesia.

● SOURCE 9

A model demonstrates the 'New Look' introduced by the fashion designer Dior in 1947.

Tasks

1   Read Sources 3 and 4. What different attitudes to married women working outside the home do these two women show?
2   Read Sources 5, 6 and 7. What attitudes to women working outside the home are shown by the men in these sources?
3   Study Sources 8 and 9. What are the 'messages' here to working women?

What was life like for most women in the 1950s?

● SOURCE 10

They're so pleased with the freshness of clothes from a <u>flameless</u> electric dryer

A typical 1950s advertisement for a clothes dryer.

Children growing up in the 1950s would find themselves surrounded by images of womanhood such as Source 10. Even school 'reading schemes' carried a similar message. The most popular reading scheme was called 'Janet and John' and invariably showed the mother doing chores around the house with Janet, her daughter, while the father and his son, John, did manly work like cleaning the car and making bonfires. Father went to work; mother stayed at home. Mother was always prettily dressed, father hard working and appreciative of home cooking and a clean house, and the children playing happily. This image of life was very much what many people wanted the 1950s to be. However, was this what it was really like? Was it like this for the women – and did they want it to be like this?

What was the impact of the war on women's work in the 1950s?

Once the war was over and men took back 'their' jobs, thousands of women were forced back into 'women's jobs' – domestic and hotel work, clerical work, nursing and shop work – or they returned to being full-time wives and mothers. All, however, had not been lost and some of the wartime gains carried over into peacetime.

- Government training courses were opened up to women who had contributed to the war effort so that they could re-train for peacetime work. However, although the government paid people allowances when they were re-training, women were paid less than men.
- More women workers joined trade unions, and most unions really did make an effort to safeguard their interests.
- The ban on married women teaching and working in the civil service was lifted.
- Medical schools were encouraged to admit women and were awarded government grants only if they admitted at least one woman for every five men. All hospital jobs were open to men and women. Scholarships were made available to women wanting a higher education in physics and chemistry, civil and electrical engineering, and aeronautical construction.
- Although the system of day nurseries that had been set up for pre-school-age children was largely disbanded after 1945 because of lack of funding, some did manage to carry on. School meals were available for all children, which went some way towards making it easier for married women to continue working, at least part-time.

Part-time work for women continued to be popular after the war. Women liked it because it gave them the opportunity to combine limited independence and a little money with their housework. Employers liked it because, at a time of full employment, it provided them with a flexible workforce who were prepared to take on mindless, repetitive jobs for low pay. Indeed, the new electrical and engineering industries did not need the brute strength of the old manufacturing industries, and increasingly employed women. By 1951, 22 per cent of married women had jobs, compared with 10 per cent before the war.

Equal pay, equal opportunities?

There was, however, one major problem for women workers: that of equal pay for equal work. Women were generally regarded as people who dipped in and out of work as they fancied. Employers, the government and, to a large extent, women themselves, believed that a girl leaving school would have a job for just a few years until she married. Then it was the husband's responsibility to look after her. Many people believed that a working wife shamed the husband, because it implied he couldn't support her. Women were not expected to hold down a job for twenty or thirty years as a man would, and so it was not thought necessary to consider appropriate pay structures for them. However, not all women agreed!

In 1951, women in teaching, the civil service and local government started a campaign for equal pay. They held marches and demonstrations, designed badges saying 'Equal pay – when?', lobbied MPs and organised petitions. Finally, in 1955, the government agreed to phase in pay increases in these three areas of work, eventually bringing women's pay up to that of men. This did not happen in other areas of work, however; neither were women regarded as equal to men when it came to promotion.

Equal opportunities were even trickier. Many people believe that equal opportunities begin at school, and with the choices you are able to make then. The 1944 Education Act established the principle of free education for all children in primary and secondary schools. Secondary schools were divided

● **SOURCE 11**

Women marching from Westminster to Trafalgar Square, London, in support of their campaign for equal pay in teaching, local government and the civil service.

into two types: grammar schools and secondary modern schools. In order to go to a grammar school, a child had to pass an examination: the 11-plus. However, the government thought that too many girls were passing the exam in comparison to boys, and in 1954 it decided to limit the number of girls who were allowed to go to grammar school. It is now estimated that, without these quotas, two-thirds of all the places in mixed grammar schools would have been occupied by girls. The quota system carried on in Birmingham and Northern Ireland until the 1980s, when it was declared illegal.

● SOURCE 12

The lives of my mother and grandmother remained unchanged. They continued to be devoted to their domestic responsibilities. But when my turn came they pushed and cajoled me through the education system and into a job market to which they believed I had every right. It never occurred to me, because of their encouragement, that I was anything other than an equal citizen. It was much later that I discovered that, even for a girl born in 1950, there was no equal access to education.

Jenni Murray, the host of BBC's *Woman's Hour*, describes her experience of equal opportunities in the school system.

● SOURCE 13

I went to the editor and said, 'Why am I not to go on doing this deputy editor's job?' He said, 'Oh, Mary, there's nothing wrong with your work, but we have to safeguard the succession and the successor has to be a man.' End message. How can you go on doing something knowing there is no promotion, knowing that young men whom you have helped to train will inevitably jump over you?

Mary Stott, working for the *Manchester Evening News,* was expecting promotion. She had been working as deputy editor every Saturday when she was suddenly dropped. This is the explanation she was given.

To work or to stay at home?

The economy was expanding rapidly in the 1950s, and there was plenty of work for those who wanted it. Single women without family responsibilities had no problems in finding a job, but they faced the problems of discrimination when it came to pay and promotion. Furthermore, married women with children faced additional problems, the most basic of which was public hostility to working mothers. In part, this arose from the following:

- the government's concern about the falling birth rate. It wanted young married women to stay at home and bring up a family. This was one of the reasons that Family Allowances had been introduced in 1947. These were payable to the mother but only for second and subsequent children
- the work of paediatrician and psychiatrist John Bowlby, who argued that it was psychologically damaging for a child to be separated from its mother for any length of time. Although he was first of all writing about children in orphanages and other institutions, his theories were expanded and applied to children living in their own homes. His book *Child Care and the Growth of Love* became a bestseller and dominated many women's thinking about how they should bring up their children.

The 'happy housewife'

Women who chose, for whatever reasons, to stay at home after marriage faced a daunting task. The first *Daily Mail* Ideal Home exhibition after the war was held in Olympia, London, in 1947 and has been held every year since. Here, the housewives of the 1950s were faced with an amazing array of gadgets designed to help them create the 'ideal' home for their husbands and children. A huge range of goods such as dusters and feather flicks, bowls and buckets, toasters and frying pans were on show, as well as cookers and fridges, electric fires and oil heaters. Whole rooms were created for demonstration purposes, and people could see the latest in, for example, furniture, wallpaper and kitchen cabinets.

Not everyone could afford these 'marvellous' gadgets and the modern approach to housework and homemaking. Washing was usually done by hand, unless there was a launderette close by. Cleaning was done with dusters and polish, mops, dustpans and brushes, carpet sweepers and carpet beaters. As the 1950s progressed, however, housework became easier.

- Clean Air Acts had reduced the pollution in the atmosphere.
- Technology produced the washing machine and vacuum cleaner, sponge mops, paper towels, detergents and a material called crimplene, which didn't need ironing.
- Mass production resulted in electrical goods becoming cheaper and, by the end of the 1950s, most homes had fridges, and many had vacuum cleaners and washing machines too.

Advertisements often came with hidden warnings as to what would happen if women didn't keep on top of their housework. In these, for example, a child was saved from bullying because his mother began washing his shirts in *Surf* washing powder, turning them from dirty grey to sparkling white; and a husband who had been tempted to stray happily returned home each night once his wife began using *Zal* disinfectant. Images of women wearing glamorous clothes, topped by a frilly apron, whisking through their housework wearing full make-up and with every hair in place, were common and were intended to persuade women that life spent at home was not drudgery. The reality, of course, was very different.

Reality, too, meant food rationing, which continued after the end of the war. It wasn't until 1954 that all food rationing finally came to an end. Tea, for example, did not come off ration until October 1952, sugar in 1953 and the last to go was meat and bacon on 4 July 1954. Even then there were still shortages and this created further stress for housewives, who often had to feed a growing family. It wasn't until well into the 1950s that shoppers could be certain that the foodstuffs they wanted would be available.

Tasks

1 Study Sources 10 and 12. How far does Source 12 challenge the view of 1950s home life shown in Source 10?
2 Draw two columns in your file. Head them 'Problems facing working women' and 'Problems facing women who stayed at home'. Work through this section and, using the information in the text and the sources, list the problems facing women in the 1950s. Which, in your view, was the most serious?

'… never had it so good'

In 1957, when Prime Minister Harold Macmillan told the British electorate that 'most of our people have never had it so good' (see Source 20), they believed him, though they knew he was trying to get their votes.

- Unemployment had stayed low throughout the 1950s, helped by women's flexible working, and at its worst it had never topped 400,000.
- More and more women were going out to work, and so many families were earning enough to pay for cars, televisions, refrigerators, electric lawn mowers and all kinds of gadgets designed to make life easier and more fun.
- Many more people than before the war began to buy their own homes.

Of course, not everyone shared in this new affluence. Many of those who didn't were often the new immigrants (see pages 48–73), who struggled to share in the material wealth enjoyed by so many.

● SOURCE 14

I wanted a rabbit, but I didn't feel like paying the 10d return on the bus to get 2/- worth of meat. I'd Wellingtons, my WVS overcoat and hooded mac on, but the cold seemed to penetrate and everyone looked pinched and cold. I paid my grocery order and left one for Monday, and got last week's and this week's eggs – four. There was a really good display of meat in the window but no one was interested – tins of gammon ham about, I should think, 1lb were 9/6, and Danish and Dutch 'minced pork in natural juices' at 4/6 and 5/6 for quite a small tin. As one woman remarked 'they don't say anything about the thick layer of fat which, with the "natural juices", made up more than half of the tin I got.'

Nella Last, a housewife living in Barrow in 1951, remembers what it was like trying to buy meat.

● SOURCE 15

I used to be up at 6.30, to get Alan and Anne-Marie ready for school. I used to take them to Mother's and start work at 7.30. When I came in on a night, I used to start straightaway, before anything, with the dinner. I used to do all me housework, washing as well, if it was washing night, in the evenings. I did a bit each night.

Mary Graham was married to a miner and took a part-time job in the late 1950s when her children started school. Her husband would not have expected to have to help with the housework, except in emergencies.

● SOURCE 16

Your home had to look absolutely scrubbed and clean and wonderful. Your children, your pram, your own appearance, every hair was sort of ironed and manicured into order because the content wasn't important. It was only the appearance. Everything was 'Ideal Home'. Whatever it was had to look nice. Everything was starched and ironed and the children had pure silk rompers. It wasn't all tumble dry and put it in the machine as it is now. It was smocking and everything took ages to wash and iron.

Carole Steyne, married in 1958, remembers what it was like to be a young housewife.

● **SOURCE 17**

Woman's Hour on the wireless was very different from what it is now. We used to be bombarded with household hints and recipes and how to do this and how to do that and we were always being sort of lectured. Housewives were always being told they must not become cabbages and bore their husbands.

A housewife remembers what the BBC radio programme *Woman's Hour* was like in the 1950s.

● **SOURCE 18**

An advertisement published in the 1950s.

● **SOURCE 19**

By the end of the 1950s we were fairly well off. We had a fridge, a car and a television. I was the only person in my class to have all three. We had a fortnight's holiday every year, usually in Cornwall where we stayed on a farm or sometimes in Frinton [Essex] where we rented a house. My mother didn't work outside the house, and she had time to join the Townswomen's Guild. She went to their classes and learned how to make silk lampshades and pewter teapot stands and jewellery. She did spend a lot of time washing, cooking and cleaning, although that wasn't too bad because she had an upright vacuum cleaner – a Hoover Junior – and when my French pen-friend came to stay in 1958, my father bought her a washing machine. It had a powered wringer and you had to be very careful not to get your fingers caught between the rubber rollers. All the time, too, she had a woman who came once a week to help her with the housework. We had quite a large garden, with a lawn, flower-beds, apple and pear trees, fruit bushes and a vegetable patch. My mother did most of the gardening, although my father always cut the grass.

Rosemary Dawson remembers family life at the end of the 1950s.

● **SOURCE 20**

Go around the country, go to the industrial towns, go to the farms and you will see a state of prosperity such as we have never had in my lifetime – nor, indeed, in the history of this country. Indeed, let us be frank about it – most of our people have never had it so good.

From a speech made by Tory Prime Minister, Harold Macmillan, in 1957.

Tasks

1. Sources 14–17 are all memories of life in the 1950s. How reliable would they be to a historian trying to find out what life was like in the 1950s? How could a historian check what they say?
2. How far do Sources 18 and 19 support what Harold Macmillan says in Source 20?

Were women discriminated against in the 1960s and early 1970s?

At first, it might seem that young women in the 'Swinging Sixties' had nothing to worry about. Called 'dolly-birds', they shocked their older relatives by their wild behaviour. Often living in bedsits or flat-shares, well away from parental control, these young women usually did secretarial work where they were chosen for the shortness of their skirts rather than their office skills. It was widely believed that, indeed, they 'never had it so good'.

● **SOURCE 21**

British designer Mary Quant in 1967 advertising the shoes she had designed.

But was it really like this for most women in the 1960s and early 1970s? What sort of freedom did they really have? How much discrimination was there against women?

The battle for equal pay

In the 1960s, women made up about one-third of the total workforce. However, although nearly half of all women aged between 20 and 64 were out working, they didn't all work all the time. Peak employment for women was between the ages of 20 and 25, and between 45 and 50. This, of course, gave a lot of support to those people who argued that women shouldn't be paid as much as men because they weren't serious about having a long-term career.

In the early 1960s, a group of industrialists, worried because women's scientific and technical training was being underused by industry, asked the London School of Economics to find out why this was. As a result, in 1968, a Royal Commission published its report into the role of women in industry. They identified three main problems:

- unequal pay: women were paid, on average, three-quarters of the salary paid to a man for doing the same job
- lack of nurseries for women with children too young to go to school
- a deeply held belief by many people that a woman's job was marriage, home-making and children, while a man's job was to go out and earn money to keep them and look after them. This denied women the opportunity for further training.

What was to be done? And who was to do it?

- In 1968, 40 women workers at the Ford factory in Dagenham, Essex, went on strike over equal pay. After a three-week strike, they settled for 92 per cent of the rate paid to male skilled workers. They then asked their union to set up a conference on discrimination against women.

- Various women's rights organisations, such as the Fawcett Society, began lobbying MPs for equal opportunities. A rally held in 1969 was attended by 30,000 people.
- The Treaty of Rome, which Britain had to sign in order to enter the Common Market (now the European Union) said that men and women had to have equal opportunities and equal pay for equal work.
- The Labour government's Secretary of State for Employment, Barbara Castle, began working towards an agreement between the government, trade unions and the CBI (Confederation of British Industry – a bosses' organisation) for equal pay for women doing the same work as men.
- In 1970 Castle introduced an Equal Pay Act into the House of Commons that was approved by both Houses of Parliament and came into full effect in 1975. This five-year gap was to let industries adapt themselves to the higher costs this legislation would involve.

Did attitudes to women's work change?

Achieving equal work for equal pay didn't necessarily mean that people's attitudes to working women, especially working married women, changed overnight. But change was coming. The opening of a whole wave of new universities in the 1960s enabled more young women to go on to higher education. This gave them more freedom and greater opportunities for following a range of different careers. No longer were women seen as simply filling in time before marriage and babies: they were beginning to be thought of as 'career girls'. Older women, too, began reaching the heights of their chosen fields of work: in 1964 Dorothy Hodgkin won the Nobel Prize for Chemistry for her research on vitamin B12, and the following year Dame Elizabeth Lane became the first woman High Court judge.

It was not all plain sailing, of course, and prejudices against women continued in many other and different ways. Women found many ways of showing just how ridiculous these prejudices were.

● SOURCE 22

In the BBC there was a strict dress code for women. In 1969 Susannah Simmons was one of that year's intake of trainee studio managers. Her pride and joy was a white polo neck sweater, white trousers and a knee-length leather jerkin. She wore them to work – ignoring the order that women should only wear trousers while on the night shift or working in the Arab section within the BBC building. A senior executive pointed out her transgression while they were both in a BBC lift, so, there and then, she took her trousers off. The rules were soon changed.

From Jenni Murray's *The Woman's Hour*, published in 1996 by the BBC.

The Sex Discrimination Act 1975

This Act established the Equal Opportunities Commission, whose main duties were to work towards the elimination of discrimination, to promote equality of opportunity between the sexes and to keep an eye on the workings of the Equal Pay Act of 1970. Of course, men could use this Act as well as women if they felt they were being discriminated against unfairly.

Task

Does Source 22 prove that there was still discrimination against women, even at the end of the 1960s? Use your own knowledge as well as the source in your answer.

What was the impact of the Women's Liberation Movement?

The Women's Liberation Movement, which began in the USA, wasn't a single organisation with membership lists, neither was it a movement for women with the same political beliefs. It was more a loose collection of events and writings, marches and conferences, group meetings and magazines that had a common theme: that of ending discrimination against women.

By the end of 1969, there were about 70 'women's lib' groups in Britain. What drove them and who supported them?

- Prominent writers such as Doris Lessing, Iris Murdoch; actresses like Vanessa Redgrave; and politicians like Barbara Castle.
- Lesser-known women, such as the fishermen's wives in Hull who campaigned for safety at sea, and the London bus conductresses who demanded the right to train as bus drivers.

The Women's Liberation Movement really began to get under way in the 1970s.

- In February 1970, the first National Women's Conference was held at Ruskin College, Oxford, and was attended by more than 500 women. They demanded equal pay, free contraception, abortion on demand and 24-hour nurseries (to enable women to work nightshifts). Later demands included the need for financial and legal independence.
- In October 1970, Germaine Greer's *The Female Eunuch* was published. It examined the ways in which men had moulded woman's psychology.
- In November 1970, the Miss World contest, held at the Royal Albert Hall in London, was disrupted by protestors shouting and throwing flour and smoke bombs. This, more than anything, brought the Women's Liberation Movement to the attention of the public.

While conferences, books and demonstrations kept women's issues in the public eye, there was also a lot going on behind the scenes. Countless small groups worked to bring about change. Women joined consciousness groups where they discussed their position in society, they set up women's refuges where women and their children were safe from abusive men, and they went out into their home towns campaigning for equal rights.

So the impact of the Women's Liberation Movement was at least two-fold. It generated a great deal of ridicule: many believed 'women's libbers' were burning their bras and hated men. On the other hand, it did a great deal to keep the issue of women's rights alive and at the forefront of people's minds.

● SOURCE 23

It was very exciting. You thought, 'This is the first time anyone's noticed this and, by God, it's going to be different tomorrow.'

Playwright Michelene Wandor, interviewed about the importance of the February 1970 National Women's Conference.

● **SOURCE 24**

I suppose I am either blamed or credited with having started the whole thing. In 1966, I and others in the US started the first Women's Liberation groups because it wasn't enough to say, 'I want to be a person.' We had to use our political power to re-structure society in a way so that women and men can move equally in the world outside the home, so that women can have a share in the decisions that affect our lives. And we must re-structure the home. Mother and father must take equal responsibility for the children. The home should no longer be a woman's world and the world outside the home can no longer be a man's world. Then there should be new social institutions like childcare centres where for some hours of the day the child can be cared for in the company of other children.

Betty Friedan, author of *The Feminine Mystique*, explains her viewpoint to Jenni Murray on the BBC programme *Woman's Hour* in 1970.

● **SOURCE 25**

The front cover of the feminist magazine *Spare Rib*, published in February 1973.

Task

What did the Women's Liberation Movement want? How did they set about getting it?

A woman's right to choose?

The most intense and angry public debates towards the end of the 1960s and in the early 1970s were not about equal pay or childcare. They were about a woman's right to choose whether or not to stay in a marriage, whether or not she was allowed to have an abortion and, combined with these, a woman's right to use a reliable contraceptive and take control of her own fertility. These issues were to have a profound effect on women's place in society: people were forced to consider how women were viewed and how women viewed themselves.

The Pill

Women, of course, are the ones who bear children, and it is this simple biological fact that has dominated a great deal of attitudes towards women and towards their work opportunities. It was argued that a reliable contraceptive, to be used by women, would enable them to take control over when, or even whether, they had children and thus give them equal access alongside men to the workplace, training and promotion.

The contraceptive pill, to be taken orally by women, was first tested in the USA in the mid-1950s, and first prescribed by British doctors in January 1961. How popular was it?

- By the summer of 1962, about 150,000 women were taking the Pill, rising to roughly 480,000 in 1964.
- A survey carried out in 1969 found that fewer than one in five women were using oral contraceptives.

Why was this? The answer is simple: access to the Pill was tightly controlled.

- In the early 1960s, most GPs would prescribe it only to married women, and the existing network of Family Planning Association clinics catered only for married couples.
- There was nowhere for single women to go until the Brook clinics opened in 1964. These began giving advice to single women and to girls as young as 16.
- It was only after the Family Planning Act of 1967 that the state really committed itself to family planning and even then it was up to local authorities to decide whether or not to open clinics. Most of the new clinics were run by the Family Planning Association, and only when they were threatened by the success of the Brook clinics did they relax their rules about seeing unmarried women.

It was only in the late 1960s and the 1970s, therefore, that the Pill became widely available to both single and married women, and began to have an impact on the sort of choices they were able to make.

● SOURCE 26

I was at university in 1968 when campus health centres were handing out the Pill like sweets. We slept around and talked a lot to each other about the evolution we were part of. And then it began to dawn. It wasn't really what we wanted, but it had become hard to say no.

An anonymous interviewee on the BBC's radio programme *Woman's Hour* in 1970, from Jenni Murray's *The Woman's Hour*, published in 1996.

The Abortion Act 1967

In the years before 1967, many women who found themselves with an unwanted pregnancy resorted to illegal abortion.

- It is estimated that in the years before 1967, around 100,000 backstreet abortions and self-induced miscarriages took place in Britain each year.
- Legal terminations were allowed in certain very limited circumstances. but the vast majority of abortions were illegal and both the pregnant woman and the person helping her could be jailed.
- Between the years 1958 and 1960, 82 women died after undergoing an illegal abortion and thousands more were hospitalised or left permanently damaged.
- In 1966, the year before the Abortion Act became law, 49 women died as the result of bungled backstreet abortions.

● **SOURCE 27**

The freedom women were supposed to have in the Sixties largely boiled down to easy contraception and abortion: things to make life easier for men, in fact.

Comment made by the journalist Julie Burchill in *The Women's Century* by Mary Turner, published in 2003.

This situation simply could not be allowed to continue indefinitely. The Abortion Law Reform Association had been set up in 1939 with a very radical agenda: one of its founder members, Stella Browne, advocated abortion on demand as a basic female right. Bills to legalise abortion were introduced in the House of Commons in 1953, 1961, 1965 and 1966. All failed.

However, public opinion was changing:

* the tragedy of deformed babies being born as a result of their mothers taking the drug thalidomide during pregnancy resulted in the Ministry of Health issuing directives in 1962 saying that 'every possible effort' should be taken to prevent such babies being born
* in 1965, the Anglican Church Assembly's Board for Social Responsibility declared that abortion could be justified if 'there was a threat to the mother's life or well-being'
* in 1967 the Liberal MP David Steel introduced the Abortion Bill that, with government support, became law at the end of the year. Abortion was possible up to the 28th week of pregnancy (later reduced to the 24th week) provided that two doctors were in agreement that it was medically or psychologically necessary.

Private clinics that charged a fee for abortion rapidly appeared throughout the country, and it was also now possible to have a free termination on the NHS. But still some people were unhappy: this was not abortion on demand, as many women wanted; and the Catholic Church and many non-Catholics remained, and still do remain, implacably opposed to abortion under any circumstances.

The Divorce Reform Act 1969

Before 1969, only the 'innocent party' in a marriage could sue for divorce. This meant, for example, that a wife could refuse her husband a divorce even though he had been gone for years, was living with another woman and had children by her. A few wives did this from spite but most acted because, before 1970, divorce was usually financially crippling for the divorced woman.

The 1969 Divorce Reform Act did away with the idea of 'innocence' and a 'guilty party'. The only grounds for divorce were the 'irretrievable breakdown' of the marriage. Furthermore, the Matrimonial Property Act of 1970 recognised that the wife's work, even if it was carried out inside the home, contributed towards the marriage and had to be taken into account in any divorce settlement.

In 1965 there had been just 2.8 divorces per 1,000 married adults in Britain; by 1990, twenty years after the Divorce Reform Act, the annual number of divorces lagged only slightly behind the annual number of marriages.

● **SOURCE 28**

The reform of the divorce laws reflected the changing role of women and the transformation of marriage from an unequal contract into a romantic partnership based on affection and companionship. Divorce reform recognised women as equal partners in a marriage.

From *White Heat: A History of Britain in the Swinging Sixties* by Dominic Sandbrook, published in 2006.

Task

To what extent do you agree with Julie Burchill (Source 27)? Use the information in this section in your answer.

How much change had taken place for women by 1975?

A great deal of change had taken place in the lives of women by 1975, as you will see from these conversations between mothers and their daughters in that year.

> I ran the home and looked after the children and your father went out and earned the money. We knew what was expected.

> But I want a career as well as marriage and children. Why can't I have both? My husband does.

> In my day we were very afraid of getting pregnant before we were married, or of having babies at the wrong time after we were married.

> Reliable contraceptives and easy abortion make it much more difficult to say 'No'. But we do have choices to make and those aren't always easy ones.

> Men should have the important managerial jobs. Who would take orders from a woman? I wouldn't feel comfortable telling a man what to do.

> I am as capable of running a company as any man! And now the law says I can't be discriminated against just because I am a woman.

> We never expected to earn what the men earned, even for doing the same work. You see, they had families to provide for, and we were just earning a bit of extra money.

> What you do with what you earn isn't the point. The point is that if you do the same work you should get the same money.

> We stayed at home and brought up our children ourselves. We didn't hand them over to strangers.

> If I stayed at home with the kids I would miss out on my career prospects. What mothers need is reliable childcare. But why should this just be the mother's problem? What about the fathers? Maybe nothing has changed!

● **SOURCE 29**

A girl of sixteen in 1970 was far more likely to remain in education than a similar sixteen-year-old in 1956. She was more likely to pursue her own intellectual and cultural interests for as long as she liked, to marry when and whom she wanted, to have children when and if she wanted, and, above all, to choose whether she remained at home as a housewife or pursued her own career.

From *White Heat: A History of Britain in the Swinging Sixties* by Dominic Sandbrook, published in 2006.

Change had come – and a great deal of very important changes had been made that affected the lives of women in the years to 1975. But change, as you will have seen from these conversations, didn't always make women's lives easier and often presented women with very difficult choices that their mothers didn't have to make.

Key points

How much change had taken place for women by 1975?

- Legislation such as the Sex Discrimination Act and the Divorce Act had improved the legal status of women.
- More women were in paid employment than in 1939 which gave them greater economic freedom but most still earned less than men.
- Women had more control over whether and when to have babies due to effective contraception and the Abortion Act.

Causes and consequences of immigration to Britain, 1939–1975

Britain has always been shaped by migration. Through history peoples have come and gone and in the process changed the country. One of the most significant periods of migration was the period 1939–1975, which laid the foundations for today's multicultural and multi-racial society in Britain. This chapter investigates this period in detail, and examines why immigrants came to Britain, what happened when they got here, and how these immigrants changed Britain.

Who came to Britain – and why?

Many people coming to live in Britain in the nineteenth and early twentieth centuries were refugees from persecution in their own countries. They came to Britain to be safe and to start a new life. But as the twentieth century progressed, people came for other reasons, too.

People came to Britain in the years after 1939 in three main waves:

- **The first wave** of immigration took place because of the Second World War and events leading up to it.

- **The second wave** took place once the war was over. Britain urgently needed a large number of workers to help rebuild the war-damaged cities, to work in the factories in order to get the peacetime economy going again, and to run London Transport and the newly introduced National Health Service. The government set up recruiting agencies in Ireland, in refugee camps and, most importantly, in the West Indies.

- **The third wave** came in the late 1960s and early 1970s. Immigration of Asian people, mainly from India and Pakistan, was the main feature of this wave.

In this chapter you will study examples from the second and third waves.

● **SOURCE 1**

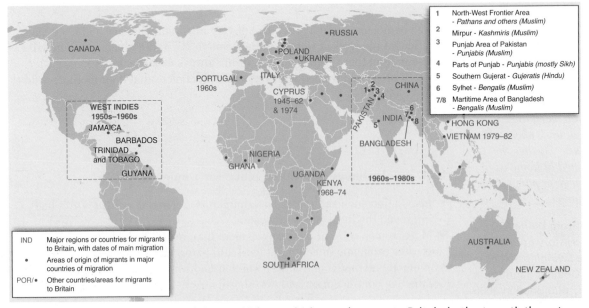

This map shows the parts of the world from which people came to Britain in the twentieth century.

Key Points

Which immigrants were living in Britain in 1945?

- Former prisoners of war, some in camps, others who chose to stay in Britain of their own free will.
- Jews, Poles and other Europeans who had fled the chaos and persecution in wartime Europe.
- Irish people, who formed the largest immigrant group in the UK throughout the twentieth century.

Wave 2: post-war immigration in the 1940s and 1950s

Following the end of the Second World War, immigration into Britain continued.

- The Irish were still the biggest group of immigrants. Nearly a million Irish people were living in Britain in the post-war period.
- Around 250,000 Caribbean people came to Britain between 1955 and 1962.
- Through the 1950s these Caribbean immigrants were joined by smaller numbers from India and Pakistan, Hong Kong and Malaysia, Cyprus and parts of Africa.

After the war ended, Britain was in desperate need of labour, both skilled and unskilled. Houses, schools, factories, railway stations and churches needed rebuilding; new government bodies, such as the National Health Service, needed skilled workers; the whole transport system, particularly London Transport, needed rebuilding and staffing. The whole economy needed re-focusing on peacetime prosperity, rather than wartime targets. Where were these workers to come from?

New arrivals came from all over Europe. These included the small number of German prisoners of war who stayed on in Britain and a larger number of refugees from the communist regimes in eastern Europe and the Soviet Union. Some 130,000 Poles, for example, arrived immediately after the ending of the war and 14,000 Hungarians came after the Soviet Union clamped down on an uprising in 1956. There were also substantial numbers of Italian labourers and a wide variety of displaced persons from refugee camps throughout Europe.

Hundreds of thousands of Irish labourers crossed the Irish Sea for what they saw as better opportunities in mainland UK. Throughout the post-war period, the Irish remained the largest immigrant community in Britain. But these European and Irish workers were still not enough to meet the demands of Britain's post-war economy.

1948: the British Nationality Act

The appeal for new workers was aimed primarily at white Europeans. However, the British Nationality Act of 1948 gave British citizenship (and therefore British passports) to the millions of citizens of British colonies, such as Hong Kong, and former colonies, such as India. This gave them the right to enter Britain and to stay for as long as they liked. The Royal Commission on Population reported in 1949 that immigrants 'of good stock' would be welcomed 'without reserve'. Employers therefore looked beyond Europe in their recruitment drive, particularly to the Caribbean. Thus began a second major wave of immigration to Britain.

Case study

SS *Empire Windrush*

The steamship SS *Empire Windrush* brought the first large group of migrant workers from the Caribbean to Britain in 1948. This event has acquired a huge symbolic significance as the first step towards the multicultural society in Britain that we now take for granted. Sources 2–7 tell you more about the people who travelled on SS *Empire Windrush*. Why did they leave their homes and lives in the Caribbean? Why did they want to come to Britain?

● SOURCE 2

Passenger Opportunity To United Kingdom

Troopship "EMPIRE WINDRUSH" sailing about 23rd MAY

Fares — Cabin Class £48

Troopdeck £28

Royal Mail Lines, Limited—8 Port Royal St.

This advertisement appeared in *The Daily Gleaner*, a Jamaican newspaper, on 13 April 1948.

The *Empire Windrush* was not part of any recruitment plan by the British government. Transport was offered simply because the ship was travelling to Britain with a half-full load and the enterprising captain wanted to fill those empty spaces. He knew there were young Jamaicans who were keen to travel to Britain to find work. When the SS *Empire Windrush* left Jamaica on 24 May 1948, it had 300 passengers below decks and 192 above. They mostly came from the British colonies of Jamaica and Trinidad.

● SOURCE 3

I came to England first in 1944 in the air force. I went back to Jamaica in 1946, but after spending two years there, it was too small for me. As a matter of fact, I had a reasonably good job in Jamaica and things were looking up. It was just a matter of the island being too small. You don't realise how small until after you've travelled. The Windrush *came in 1948 and I returned to England and to more freedom.*

Arthur Curling explains why he decided to come to Britain on SS *Empire Windrush*.

● SOURCE 4

I first came to England during the war, in the RAF. I was in the war for three years. When I went back home there was no work so I decided to come back. There was a boat coming back, by the name of Windrush, *and it was only £28 so I paid my fare and came back. The opportunity for jobs in England was better than back home in Jamaica.*

Clinton Edwards explains why he returned to England after the war.

● SOURCE 5

I came here in 1948 because my husband sent for me. He and his brother came over a year before. I reached here on 22 June. It was a lovely day, beautiful, and they were at the dock waiting for me. I think it was Tilbury. I was very excited. I was coming to meet my husband. I was very anxious to come and meet him because when he left we were just married. We got married and he left the following day. Jamaica in 1948 was all right to me. If my husband had not sent for me I would not have come at that point. Maybe later.

Lucile Harris explains why she was a passenger on the *Windrush*.

● SOURCE 6

I was born in Jamaica in 1926. The 'mother country' was at war with Nazi Germany and I did believe in the British Empire and as a young man I volunteered to contribute and fight Nazi Germany. A lot of people don't realise that Britain stood alone for nearly two years against tyranny. We as part of the former British Empire volunteered and contributed and I am glad we did that. I have been here during the war fighting Nazi Germany and I came back to help build Britain.

Sam King explains why he wanted to go to Britain on the *Windrush*.

Settling in

On their arrival in Britain, many like Lucile (Source 5) went to stay with friends or relatives. There were 236 passengers who had nowhere to live and these were temporarily housed in a shelter in south-west London that had previously been used for holding German and Italian prisoners of war. It was less than a mile from the nearest labour exchange in Coldharbour Lane, Brixton, and many Jamaicans went there to find out what jobs were available in the locality. Of those 236 passengers, 202 found jobs straightaway; many in the new National Health Service, but most with London Transport, helping to run the trains and the buses.

The political debate

While the SS *Empire Windrush* was on its way to Tilbury Docks in London, a furious debate was taking place in Parliament.

Some MPs disapproved of the Nationality Act (see page 49). They said that the *Windrush*'s passengers had no right to come to live and work in Britain, and that they ought to be turned away on arrival. They feared that allowing the immigrants to disembark set a dangerous precedent – that with literally millions of people having the right to settle in Britain the country could be swamped with new arrivals.

Others argued that many of the passengers were ex-servicemen who had fought for Britain during the Second World War and that therefore a debt of gratitude was owed to them. They argued that they were only likely to stay for a year, that the British economy needed all the workers it could find, and that as the passengers had British passports they couldn't be turned away anyway.

The 'welcomers' won the day, but this disagreement set the terms of the debate about immigration that would continue through the next two decades. The debate was not only about 'immigration', it was also about 'race'. Did Britain want, and could it cope with, mass immigration from Asia and the Caribbean?

● SOURCE 7

Passengers on board SS *Empire Windrush* at Tilbury docks, London, on 22 June 1948. An RAF recruiting officer is speaking to men who want to join the airforce.

Tasks

1   Historians talk about 'push' factors that make people want to leave somewhere, and 'pull' factors that attract people to a particular place. Make a list of the push and pull factors mentioned in the case study and sources.

2   Read Sources 3–6. Are the 'push' or 'pull' factors more important in the decisions made by Arthur, Clinton, Lucile and Sam?

Why did Caribbean immigration increase during the 1950s?

Most *Windrush* immigrants *did* quickly and successfully settle in Britain. They had come to Britain to improve their prospects and that is what happened. They earned money and were able to send some home. For many employers, too, immigration was a perfect solution to their problems – they welcomed this supply of eager, hard-working young people.

You might expect the success of the *Windrush* immigrants to have attracted a flood of further immigrants from the West Indies. At the time many British people expected that as well, particularly because they knew that life was very hard for many people in the British colonies. The British government investigated living conditions in the Caribbean and found that most people faced poor housing, poor wages, poor healthcare and a poor education system. The economy had been devastated by two bad hurricanes and the sugar trade (which was the main source of income) was very depressed. There was a long tradition of migrant work among young West Indians.

However, the cost of sailing to the UK was still too high for most people in the Caribbean and in those days flying was even more expensive. They also had an alternative outlet much closer to home – young West Indians were much more likely to move to the USA to work. So in 1949 and 1950 there were only a few hundred arrivals from the Caribbean each year and these went largely unremarked.

Two developments helped change this pattern:

- in 1952 the USA put severe restrictions on immigration (from 65,000 down to only 800 a year), which reduced opportunities for workers from the Caribbean
- in 1956 London Transport (who had been recruiting West Indians for some years) started a scheme in which they paid for the migrants' boat fare and the workers paid it back gradually over the coming months out of their earnings.

In the following years migration from the West Indies rose steadily, as you can see from Source 9. About a quarter of a million Caribbean people settled in Britain between 1955 and 1972.

By the late 1950s money being sent by workers in Britain was the second largest source of income for the island of Jamaica. Having a family member in Britain was a source of pride. And the money sent home allowed families to buy luxuries such as a fridge or a flushing toilet.

● SOURCE 8

I lost my job late in 1952 and stayed unemployed for over a year. I thought and thought and could not invent anything else but to migrate. I was fatherless and at one time or other the only provider for my family. Migration to the UK seemed to me to be an urgent necessity. I could then support my mother and younger brothers. I could pay off her mortgage and everything would be all right.

Wallace Collins, in his book *Jamaican Migrant*, published in 1965, explains his reasons for leaving Jamaica.

● **SOURCE 9**

Period	West Indies	Asian	Other	Total
1948–53	14,000	4,000	10,000	28,000
1954	11,000	1,300	5,700	18,000
1955	27,500	7,600	7,600	42,700
1956	29,800	7,600	9,540	46,940
1957	23,000	11,800	7,600	42,400
1958	15,000	10,900	3,950	29,850
1959	16,400	3,800	1,400	21,600
1960	49,650	8,400	0	58,050
1961	66,300	48,850	0	115,150
1962 (to June)	27,000	43,000	13,700	83,700

Government estimates of the number of Commonwealth immigrants to the UK, 1948–62, and area of origin.

Tasks

1 Which of the following statements are supported or challenged by the sources and text? Explain why.
   a) Immigration rose steadily through the 1950s.
   b) Caribbean migration always exceeded Asian migration in the 1950s.
   c) All young men were desperate to leave the West Indies.
2 Which of Sources 8 and 9 do you think is the more useful for investigating why Caribbean immigration increased in the 1950s?

Wave 3: immigration in the 1960s and 1970s

The 1960s and '70s saw some significant changes in terms of immigration.

- In 1962 the government introduced a law that put severe limits on the number of Commonwealth immigrants allowed into Britain (see Source 9 on page 53).
- The nature of immigration began to change. In the 1950s most immigrants had been single men coming to Britain who did not necessarily intend to settle. From the 1960s onwards immigrants were increasingly women and children joining family members already in this country. They intended to settle in Britain for good.
- The other big difference in this period was that immigration from India and Pakistan outpaced immigration from the Caribbean. The steady stream of Asian migrants was boosted by two particular events which meant that 71,000 Asians living in Kenya and Uganda were forced to leave. The main influx of Kenyan Asians was in 1967 and of Ugandan Asians in 1972.
- However, throughout this period more people left Britain than came. They were in search of what they thought would be a better life in countries such as Canada and Australia. These countries encouraged emigration of white people from Britain by offering inducements like cheap fares.

Background: Asian migration in the 1950s

The Nationality Act of 1948 gave the right to live and work in Britain to many millions of people in India. After India gained independence in 1948, the country was split in two: India and Pakistan. The partition led to extreme violence and many communities were badly affected. Some groups, particularly Sikhs from the Punjab region, took this opportunity to seek refuge in Britain. They headed largely for the West Midlands, and many came to work in engineering.

Asian migration continued through the 1950s (see Source 9). Although often lumped together as 'Indians' by the white British, the Asian migrants were in fact from a wide variety of countries, backgrounds and religions. They spoke different languages and had different customs. There were, for example, Hindus from Gujarat, Sikhs from the Punjab and Muslims from Pakistan.

Some Asian migrants were highly-educated professionals or enormously successful business people in their home countries. Others were rural labourers who had never been to a major city. For example, a large number of people were displaced during the period 1961–67 by the building of the Mirpur dam in Kashmir and spent their compensation money on a one-way ticket to Britain.

This varied pattern continued in the 1960s. However, the two most significant waves of Asian immigration were not from the Indian subcontinent at all but from Africa. And in most cases they were definitely pushed rather than pulled!

● **SOURCE 10**

For everyone in India life was a struggle to earn his daily bread. Those who are employed by others sweat to earn 100 rupees or even 200 – seldom more. With that wage they have to keep their families for a whole month. On the other hand, I saw for myself those people who had been to England come back wearing brand new suits and loaded with money. And all those who had daughters to marry would rush to their doors. Those who had been to England to work could send money home each month and still afford to buy land or build a fine house in India on their return. Surely if they could do all this, I could do the same.

From *Rampal and his Family* by Ursula Sharma, published in 1971.

● **SOURCE 11**

In 1962 I left Pakistan and went to Nottingham. I knew I wasn't going to get any better job than being a British Railway cleaner. I had seen qualified people from my country who had been teachers and barristers and none of them got proper work. They were labourers, bus conductors and railway cleaners like me. Many times we could read and write much better than the people who were in charge of us. They knew I had been a Customs Inspector in Pakistan, but that didn't matter.

A Pakistani immigrant comments in the late 1980s
about his experiences in the 1960s.

Why did Kenyan Asians come to Britain in 1967?

Asians, mainly from India, had been migrating to East Africa since the mid-nineteenth century. Initially working on railway construction programmes, many stayed and over the years became central to their adopted country's prosperity. They worked, for example, in business and industry and as bankers and insurers. Then things began to change.

Kenya was a British colony. When it gained independence in 1963, over 100,000 Asians were living there. The new Kenyan government, led by their Prime Minister, Jomo Kenyatta, gave the Asians a choice. They could either become Kenyan or remain British but they could not be both: 95,000 of them decided to stay British and so kept their British passports.

Asians in Kenya had long faced resentment. They were generally more successful and had higher incomes than most black Kenyans. This resentment grew and finally, in 1967, the government declared that all non-Kenyan Asians were foreigners and could only stay and work on a temporary basis. Fearing the worst, many fled. Since they had British passports they came to Britain.

● **SOURCE 12**

Immigration laws in Kenya are becoming increasingly severe. Foreigners can only hold a job until a Kenyan national can be found to replace them, and more and more cities, including Nairobi [the capital city] are demanding that the government bans non-Kenyans from owning a shop or trading in municipal markets. If the Kenyan government caves in to such demands, the result is likely to be chaos, as most shops are owned by foreigners, and not enough citizens have the capital or knowledge to run small businesses. Already the tens of thousands of Asians, who until now have dominated commerce, industry and most key jobs in the country, are finding their lives made impossible. They are now arriving [in Britain] at the rate of more than 1,000 a month to start a new life in the UK, a country which most have never seen.

A BBC news broadcast, 4 February 1968.

● **SOURCE 13**

Only Kenyan citizens are being allowed work permits. I was forced to sell my fleet of lorries and come to Britain to look for a new life.

Omar Sharmar explains why he left Kenya in 1968. He had a haulage business in Mombasa that he was forced to close when the government wouldn't give him a licence.

● **SOURCE 14**

We did find some difficulty in filling the planes until last week. But in the last two or three days that has all changed, and there doesn't seem to be any difficulty at all now. At the present rate I think this will continue for at least a year, if not more.

An airline official in Nairobi, February 1968.

This was one of the most high-profile immigrations to Britain. In 1967, 1,000 Kenyan Asians began to arrive in Britain every week and the TV cameras were there to greet them. In all, 20,000 Kenyans arrived until in 1968 the government put a limit on how many could come. This immigration was controversial and had political consequences (see pages 66–69).

What happened in Uganda?

Four years later, a very similar scenario was played out in Uganda (see Source 15).

What had happened to make the president of a country issue such a warning? As had been the case in Kenya, the Asian community had played a large part in building up Uganda's economy. By the late 1960s Uganda was one of the most prosperous countries in Africa. However, as with Kenya, resentment was building up among Uganda's black African population.

Matters came to a head when Idi Amin asked Britain for financial help and was refused. In August 1972, Amin condemned the entire Asian population of Uganda as 'bloodsuckers' and issued a decree expelling them. All 60,000 of them had to be gone within 90 days. Amin believed Britain would have to take them in and many people saw this as a retaliatory action against Britain for not giving aid to Uganda. Amin then had a slight change of mind and issued a second decree. This second decree stated that all professionals (doctors, lawyers and teachers, for example) had to stay and that if any of them tried to leave, they would be committing treason.

The British tried to negotiate a compromise deal, but failed. They then offered the Ugandan Asians a choice of an Indian or British passport. The majority chose British, believing Britain would offer greater stability and security if they had to leave. In the end, almost 27,000 Ugandan Asians flew into Britain with nothing more than what they could carry.

● **SOURCE 15**

I will make you feel as if you are sitting on fire. Your main interest has been to exploit the economy for years and now I say to you all – GO!

Part of a warning given by Idi Amin, President of Uganda, in August 1972 to the Asians living there.

● **SOURCE 16**

[I,] my wife, two daughters and my sister had to buy our tickets out of the country, and were only allowed to leave with £54 in our pockets – there was no free exit. We could see soldiers all around our house. It was very frightening. We drove to Entebbe airport at night, and managed to avoid the police checkpoints because if they had discovered me leaving I would have been detained, as I was considered one of the professional classes. We left our car at the airport and boarded our British Caledonian flight at about 11 o'clock at night and it was only when we were flying over Kenyan airspace that we drew a sigh of relief. We were happy to leave, but sad to leave in such a way. Our pockets were all but empty, but we had an education and we were determined to re-start our lives.

Sharm Karnik, who was a young headteacher in the Ugandan capital, Kampala, in 1972, remembers how he and his immediate family got out.

● **SOURCE 17**

On the way to the airport, the coach was stopped by troops seven times and we were all held at gunpoint.

Kassem Osman, an Asian Ugandan, describes what happened to him and his brothers as they tried to get to the airport.

● **SOURCE 18**

I had a £250 gold watch taken off my wrist while I was on my way to Entebbe airport and every piece of Ugandan money stolen from my wallet.

A retired government clerk from Kampala describes what happened to him on his way to the airport.

● **SOURCE 19**

We know many of you didn't really want to leave your homes and jobs in Uganda. You know we didn't really want you to come before, because we have problems with homes and jobs here. But most of us believe that this is a country that can use your skills and energies ... You will find that we, like other countries, have our bullies and misfits. We are particularly sorry about those of our politicians who are trying to use your own troubles for their own ends. And we're glad that your British passport means something again.

The front page of the *Economist* magazine, 19 August 1972.

● SOURCE 20

'Departheid'. A cartoon by Keith Waite for the *Daily Mirror*, published 19 December 1972.

Tasks

1   Were the Asians expelled from Kenya and Uganda for the same reasons?
2   Kenyan and Ugandan Asians faced enormous problems leaving Africa. To what extent were they the same problems? Use the sources in your answer.

Key points

Why did different groups migrate to Britain between 1948 and 1972?

- Different groups came for different reasons.
- The Nationality Act 1948 extended British citizenship to all people in the British Empire.
- Economic hardship, political turmoil and natural disasters in their home country all served to make Britain an attractive place for migrants.
- Governments and private companies recruited workers to help rebuild Britain.
- In the early period immigrants were largely single men coming to make money to send home. In the later period immigrants were increasingly women and children coming to Britain to join their families.

What were the experiences of immigrants to Britain?

A wide range of immigrant groups came to Britain and their experiences varied enormously. What life was like for immigrants depended on:

- where they lived
- when they came
- what their skills were
- what ethnic group they belonged to.

The experience of West Indian immigrants in the 1950s

Most Caribbean immigrants came to Britain with high expectations. They were coming to their mother country which they admired. Many were coming at the invitation of the British government or organisations who needed them. However, far from being welcomed, West Indian immigrants often quickly came face to face with racial discrimination and what at that time was called the 'colour bar'. During the war black soldiers had been greeted warmly in many communities around Britain and people had prided themselves that black GIs were treated as equals here and that Britain was less racist than the USA. However in peacetime things were different. The underlying attitudes of racial superiority and suspicion of foreigners – particularly 'coloured' foreigners – that had existed in the British Empire for centuries re-emerged. The result for many immigrant people in Britain was an overwhelming feeling that they were not welcome. This affected three aspects of life in particular.

1. Housing

It would be illegal nowadays, but in the 1950s it was common for boarding houses to put up a notice saying 'No blacks' or 'No coloureds'. If asked, the landlord or landlady might say that they themselves were not prejudiced but that they had to 'think of the neighbours' or the other tenants who would not want to live alongside a black person.

Most West Indian immigrants were intending to stay only a short time in Britain. They did not intend to buy property – and in any case banks and building societies would not give new immigrants loans or mortgages. They could not get council houses because you had to live in Britain for five years before you could even apply. So they had to take whatever rented accommodation they could get and this tended to be low-quality housing in inner-city areas that no one else wanted. Much of it was in areas still ruined from wartime bombing. New immigrants were often vulnerable to exploitation. For example, one unscrupulous property developer called Peter Rachman owned over 100 properties in West London. He got rid of the local white residents (sometimes with the threat of violence) then subdivided the houses into many units and packed them with young immigrants who had to pay inflated rents.

Immigrants who arrive in a new country usually tend to choose to live with others from their own country; that is human nature. The difficulty in finding housing increased this tendency. As a result, West Indian communities were focused in particularly poverty-stricken areas of London – Jamaicans in Brixton, Trinidadians and Barbadians in Notting Hill and Paddington, Guyanese in Tottenham. Outside London, similar Caribbean communities grew up in Moss Side (Manchester), Handsworth (Birmingham) and Chapeltown (Leeds).

● SOURCE 21

It was shocking, the accommodation ... You go along some part in Nottingham you would see signs put up, 'Rooms for rent, no niggers need apply', that's not unusual ... I described the conditions of the houses ... they pack as much people as they can in these houses and charge them, at the time, very, very high rent. It was very, very bad.

From an interview with Connie Mark, in the book *Windrush* written by Mike Phillips and Trevor Phillips, 1999.

● SOURCE 22

Black workers outside the employment exchange in London, 1948. The exchange was in a refitted air-raid shelter.

2. Jobs

Most immigrants found it easy to find a job but they faced a number of problems in the workplace.

- In many cases, the jobs they found were not suited to their skills. One survey found that half the West Indians in London in the late 1950s were over-qualified for the job they were doing, though the pay was better than they could have got at home.
- Many immigrants found that it was hard to get on in their careers. For example, black nurses in the NHS were discouraged from gaining qualifications that would have enabled them to be promoted. Also, many immigrants did not apply for jobs that they were qualified for because they knew they would not be seriously considered by employers.
- Immigrant workers also faced opposition from trade unions and from white colleagues who viewed them as a threat. In 1955 transport workers in the West Midlands went on strike to protest about the 'increasing numbers of coloured workers' (in the case of West Bromwich, this actually meant one Indian bus conductor). The Transport and General Workers Union demanded that no more than five per cent of bus drivers could be black. In 1958 the Trades Union Congress passed a resolution calling for an end to all immigrant workers entering the country.
- Finally, to make matters worse, opponents of immigration accused immigrants of coming to Britain to cash in on the benefit system. This was in spite of the fact that most immigrants were in employment and many had come to Britain in the first place at the government's request because there was a shortage of British workers.

3. Leisure

In the early 1950s, two-thirds of West Indian immigrants were single young men. They had a great deal of leisure time on their hands. As well as being attracted by the money, they had come to Britain for adventure and excitement. However, they found the 'colour bar' affected their leisure time as well.

Tasks

1 The written sources on pages 59–61 describe different experiences of immigration. On your own or with others write a headline summing up the key point in each source. Make it as short as you can. For example, Source 23 could be headlined: 'Please don't come to this church again!'

2 Sources 25–28 could be interpreted in different ways: as examples of prejudice or examples of kindness and welcome. Choose one and explain how it could be used both ways.

Some pubs banned black drinkers. Others gave such a frosty reception that immigrants would not dream of going there. Instead they would go to a (usually unlicensed) drinking club. This 'solution' then became part of another problem, as these clubs acquired a reputation for loud music, prostitution, gambling and fighting. In reality most were simply a place for young men who lived in overcrowded accommodation to meet with friends and relax, but in places like Notting Hill the clubs added to the tension between white and black residents.

A sober church-going young man might find the 'colour bar' in operation even in the churches, although there were exceptions to this depressing rule.

● SOURCE 23

Biggest shock of all was, one, the cold, and two, having gone to church for the very first time – so delighted that I'm coming from an Anglican church back home, I went to join in the worship, and so I did – but after the service I was greeted by the vicar, who politely and nicely told me: 'Thank you for coming. But I would be delighted if you didn't come back ... My congregation is uncomfortable in the company of black people.' That was the biggest shock. I was the only black person in that congregation that morning, and my disappointment, my despair went with me. I didn't say anything to anyone about it for several months after that.

Carmel Jones describes his experiences when he came to Britain in 1955. He went on to become a Pentecostal minister.

Carmel Jones (Source 23) mentions his disappointment at the colour bar. Many West Indians had high hopes of Britain and had admired it from a distance. Yet for many it proved so much less impressive than they had expected. They put up with it for the sake of the weekly pay packet and the money to send home, but that was about all.

● SOURCE 24

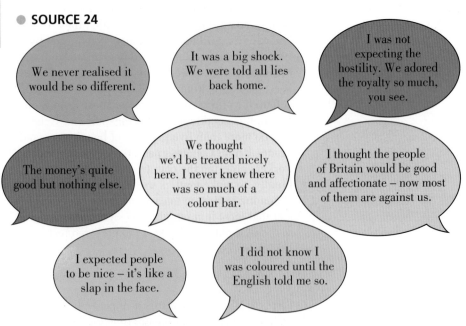

We never realised it would be so different.

It was a big shock. We were told all lies back home.

I was not expecting the hostility. We adored the royalty so much, you see.

The money's quite good but nothing else.

We thought we'd be treated nicely here. I never knew there was so much of a colour bar.

I thought the people of Britain would be good and affectionate – now most of them are against us.

I expected people to be nice – it's like a slap in the face.

I did not know I was coloured until the English told me so.

These statements are drawn from interviews in the 1960s conducted by Daniel Lawrence, who asked West Indian immigrants about their experiences of Britain.

Of course, these negative experiences are not the whole story. They were widespread, yet there were other people who found a warm welcome and a positive experience. For most, the experience of coming to Britain was a combination of many different and complicated feelings, as summed up by Ivan Weekes in Source 25 below.

● SOURCE 25

I used to feel not only frightened but wondering what is going to happen next. I could get bumped off. And people would look at you, like spears, daggers. People would spit at you. Nobody spat at me personally but I know what happened. If you went to sit down beside somebody on a bus they'd shuffle up. But then somebody would look at you, see that you are frightened as hell and say, 'Oh mate, take no notice of them, we're not all the same.' I think that's so important to say. That was my experience: 'Take no notice of them, we're not all the same.' And just those few words gave me two things: hope and comfort. People were not all the same.

Ivan Weekes, who came to Britain in 1955.

● SOURCE 26

Jamaicans' friend leaving Wolverhampton
Rev Howard Belben, minister of Darlington Street Methodist Church in Wolverhampton, is moving to Sheffield. Mr Belben has taken great interest in Wolverhampton's Jamaican population. He has married many Jamaican couples and has baptised several Jamaican babies. Untiring in his efforts to help Jamaicans he has been in regular contact with about 300 of them.

An extract from the *Wolverhampton Express and Star*, 1957.

● SOURCE 27

I was in love with Britain and that love only grew when I came here from the Caribbean in the 1950s. I was employed by the National Health Service as a midwife. I loved the clean hospitals, the efficiency and order. I hated the disorder I had left behind. But my feelings of pride and love were beaten down again and again by racism, ignorance and abuse. There was such unfairness to us Christian people who fought in the war with the best of them.

A West Indian woman being interviewed in the late 1990s.

● SOURCE 28

People talk about a colour problem arising in Britain. How can there be a colour problem here? Even after all the immigration of the past few years, there are only 190,000 [coloured] people in our population of over 50 million – that is only four out of every 1,000. The real problem is not black skins but white prejudice.

Comments made by a delegate at the TUC Conference in 1958.

Key points

What were the experiences of immigrants?

- Racial discrimination was common and affected immigrants' experience of housing, employment, and leisure activity.
- Some immigrants had high expectations of Britain and were deeply disappointed by the reality.
- Immigrants tended to live with others from their own country, which gave them much needed support.
- Although the government had invited immigrants over to Britain to work, they were actually given less practical help to settle than even the German prisoners of war who settled here after the war.

1958: summer of violence

By 1958 there were over 200,000 people from the New Commonwealth living in Britain. This was still a tiny percentage of the British population. If you were a white Briton living in rural England you might never see a 'coloured' immigrant. You might not even be aware of immigration at all. But if you lived in Brixton or Notting Hill in London it might be all around you. It was these city areas that saw an outbreak of racial violence in 1958.

The previous pages show that racial discrimination and prejudice was widespread in Britain but it had not usually spilled into violence. What had changed?

- There was an economic downturn after years of growth so jobs were scarcer – some white people blamed the immigrants for 'taking their jobs'.
- A new gang culture was emerging among white youths, epitomised by the 'Teddy Boys' (see page 4).

Nottingham

There were a number of attacks on black people living in Nottingham, including a black miner who was beaten up as he came out of a cinema with his wife. Black people felt increasingly unsafe walking around the streets of Nottingham. Events came to a head on 23 August 1958 when fighting broke out for over an hour between groups of whites and blacks in the St Ann's Well Road area. One response to this violence was that the MPs for Nottingham called for an end to black immigration to Britain.

Notting Hill

Notting Hill had one of the largest West Indian communities in Britain. The right-wing Union Movement, a fascist organisation led by Oswald Mosley, had been involved in racist attacks against Jewish immigrants in the 1930s. They tried to exploit the growing resentment against coloured immigrants and set up an office in Notting Hill producing leaflets calling for people to 'Take Action Now ... Protect Your Jobs ... Stop Coloured Immigration ... Homes for White People'. The leaflets even featured pictures of black people with spears entering Britain.

Then, in late August 1958, gangs of around 400 Teddy Boys and other white youths launched two nights of attacks on black people and their property. They petrol-bombed some houses.

● SOURCE 29

Within half an hour the mob ... had broken scores of windows and set upon two negroes who were lucky to escape with cuts and bruises. Women from top floor windows laughed as they called down to the thousand strong crowd, 'Go on boys, get yourself some blacks'.

From an interview with Ivan Weekes in the book *Windrush* written by Mike Phillips and Trevor Phillips, 1999.

The black population received no protection from the police. However, on the third night they fought back and at that stage police intervened to stop the fighting. Many arrests were made.

● SOURCE 30

You are a minute and insignificant section of the population who have filled the whole nation with horror, indignation and disgust. Everyone, irrespective of the colour of their skin, is entitled to walk through our streets in peace, with their heads held up and free from fear.

Statement by the judge sentencing four white youths convicted of involvement in the Notting Hill violence of August 1958.

● SOURCE 31

"*Go on, boy! I may have lost that war, but my ideas seem to be winning . . .*"

Cartoon that appeared in the *Daily Mirror* on 2 September 1958.

Tasks

1 Study Source 31. Why was this cartoon published on 2 September 1958?
2 What is the message of Source 31?
3 How reliable is Source 31 as an indicator of what people in Britain thought of the racial violence of 1958? You can refer to other sources in your answer if you wish.

The murder of Kelso Cochrane

In May 1959, Kelso Cochrane, a carpenter from Antigua, was stabbed to death in Notting Hill by six white youths on his way home from a hospital appointment in nearby Paddington. The police never arrested the killers and they were accused of not doing enough. Twelve hundred people turned up at Cochrane's funeral (Source 32) to show their anger and sorrow at what had happened.

● SOURCE 32

The funeral of Kelso Cochrane, 11 June 1959.

Consequences

The violence was widely condemned – see Sources 30 and 31 – and most British people were appalled by it. We need to remember that such violence was the exception rather than the norm. It was precisely because it was so shocking and unexpected that it caused such a stir. Remember too that there are many examples of local white people protecting their black neighbours, even during the violence in Notting Hill in August 1958.

When BBC reporters spoke to the local population in Notting Hill, almost all the white and black people interviewed said positive things about their black or white neighbours. They blamed the violence on a tiny minority of black people, who gave the immigrants a bad name, and white people intent on stirring up hatred in order to reduce immigration. On the other hand the black community felt that the police had not protected them from violence. This distrust of the police among the Caribbean community persisted through the following decades.

The violence affected the future of immigration and race-relations in Britain in two main ways.

- Immigration became a national political issue and the heated debate was focused mostly around race. The question was not 'Does Britain need immigrants?' but 'Does Britain want New Commonwealth (i.e. coloured) immigrants?' Although politicians officially condemned the racist attitudes that stirred up the violence, from this point on all political parties developed policies that limited New Commonwealth immigration (see page 66).

- On the other hand, many people woke up to the fact that racism itself needed tackling. Some local communities took positive action to build better relationships between black and white communities. As a direct response to the violence, the St Pancras carnival was set up in 1959 and later moved onto the streets to become the Notting Hill Carnival (see Source 34). However it was another seven years before the government brought in laws to outlaw racial discrimination (see page 66).

● **SOURCE 34**

Claudia Jones arriving at Southampton in 1955.

Claudia Jones came to London in 1955 after being deported from America for her activities in the Communist Party. Shortly after her arrival she set up the West Indian Gazette, the first newspaper for the West Indian community in Britain. After the Notting Hill riots in 1958, Jones and some of her colleagues on the newspaper decided that they wanted to provide a positive focus for the community and set up the first Carnival to celebrate West Indian dance, music and culture. In January 1959 the first indoor Carnival was held in St Pancras, London, attracting 7,000 people. The slogan was 'A people's art is the genesis of their freedom'. It moved to Notting Hill in later years and has become the biggest street party in Europe.

● **SOURCE 33**

"We must pretend it doesn't exist"

THE IMMIGRATION ISSUE

Cummings

Cartoon from the *Daily Express*, 24 August 1961. Labour leader Harold Wilson (left) is talking to Conservative leader Sir Alec Douglas-Home (right).

The Asian experience

Asian immigrants settled particularly in the textile towns of Yorkshire and Lancashire. By 1971, for example, ten per cent of the population of Bradford was Pakistani. They also settled in the East and West Midlands and in areas of London such as Southall and Newham. One of the largest communities of all was in Leicester. Through the 1970s its Asian population quadrupled. By 1981 the city was officially the most 'non-white' city in Britain: nearly a quarter of the population came from Asian backgrounds.

In many ways the Asian experience was similar to that of Caribbean migrants, described on pages 58–63. On the other hand, there were some important differences:

- whereas Caribbean immigrants has mostly regarded themselves as British – and many idolised the mother country before they came to Britain – very few Asians did (see Source 35). Asians, it seems, had much lower expectations of Britain. Indeed many had been warned that Britain was a wicked place full of drunks and failed marriages. If they had low expectations they were less likely to be disappointed
- there was often a language barrier that added to the racial barriers that already existed. Whereas nearly all West Indians spoke English, many Asians – particularly women – did not and some did not learn it even when they got to Britain
- even when they had come to settle in Britain, many Asian immigrants did their utmost to keep their links to their home country. For many, the patterns of marriage and family life continued as it had in their country of origin and single men often went back home to find a bride
- many Asians tended to keep themselves to themselves – a very British habit – which exposed them less to abuse or discrimination. Their lives and entertainment were focused around the home and the community or the religious place of worship
- many Asians went into business – for example, owning their own shop or restaurant. They did not therefore suffer first-hand discrimination at work from their colleagues or employers, although many did from their customers
- one of the most remarkable features of Asian immigration was the success of many migrants in business, although many Asian immigrants remained very poor.

● **SOURCE 35**

Findings from an investigation in Nottingham in the 1960s.

	Jamaicans	Indians and Pakistanis
Did you feel British before you came to Britain?	Yes 87%	Yes 2%
Is it fine with you if your children feel English?	Yes 86%	Yes 6%

The political response to immigration

Immigration was a tricky issue for politicians of all parties. They had to balance the interests of:

- the economy – employers depended on immigrant labour
- the voters – the politicians had to keep their voters happy and they knew that the majority of British people were anti-immigration
- immigrants themselves – immigrant communities needed the protection of the law just as much as non-immigrant communities
- the need to prevent racial tension in Britain's cities.

At different times policy was driven more by one or other of these demands. The table below summarises the government measures that were introduced.

Government measures 1962–1976

Date	Government measure	Notes
1962	The **Commonwealth Immigrants Act 1962** introduced a voucher system. Only immigrants with a valuable skill or who could do a job where there was a shortage of workers could get a voucher.	Although it did not specifically say so, the Act was aimed at restricting the influx of immigrants from Asia and the West Indies because a greater proportion of them tended to be unskilled. One effect of this Act was to increase immigration in the short term. In 1961 more than 130,000 people came to Britain in order to get in before the 1962 Act took effect. That was more than in the previous five years put together! The same pattern repeated itself over the next 15 years – each time a restriction was introduced, a large number of people rushed into Britain to beat it.
1965–66	The **Race Relations Act 1965** made it illegal to discriminate against any person because of their colour or race. In 1966 the **Race Relations Board** was set up to handle complaints about discrimination.	However, the Board had no powers to enforce its decisions.
1968	The **Commonwealth Immigrants Act 1968** reduced the number of work vouchers and introduced a 'close connection' qualification. It was no longer enough to have a British passport, you also had to be born in Britain, or have parents or grandparents who were born in Britain.	This favoured immigrants from Commonwealth countries such as Canada, Australia or New Zealand. It was particularly aimed at preventing the entry of large numbers of Kenyan Asians (see page 56).
1968	The **Race Relations Act 1968** made discrimination in areas such as housing and employment illegal.	However, an employer could still discriminate indirectly – for example, by claiming that another candidate had more experience.
1976	The **Race Relations Act 1976** made racially offensive music or publications illegal. It also set up tribunals so that any job applicant who felt he or she was suffering from discrimination could report the employer. In addition, it set up the Commission for Racial Equality to investigate and combat racism.	

Integration and anti-discrimination

In 1966 Roy Jenkins, the Home Secretary in the Labour government – the person most responsible for immigration policy – made an important speech to the National Committee for Commonwealth Immigrants (see Source 36). For the first time, he acknowledged that many of the immigrants who now lived in Britain had decided to make it their home, rather than seeing Britain as a place where they would stay for a few years before returning back to their country of origin. He argued that, as a consequence of this change, both the host society (the majority of people in Britain) and the immigrants and ethnic minorities had to work together to achieve a successful form of integration. In other words, it was a two-way process.

At the same time organisations such as CARD were established to expose racial discrimination (see Source 37).

● SOURCE 36

Integration is perhaps a loose word. I do not regard it as meaning the loss, by immigrants, of their own characteristics and culture. I do not think we need in this country a 'melting pot', which will turn everybody out in a common mould, as one would a series of carbon copies of someone's misplaced version of the stereotyped Englishness. I define integration, therefore, as not a flattening process of assimilation [everyone becoming the same] but equal opportunity accompanied by cultural diversity in an atmosphere of mutual tolerance.

From a speech by Roy Jenkins, Home Secretary in the Labour government, 1966.

● SOURCE 37

No CARD member will need to be told that racial discrimination is widespread in Britain, especially in jobs, housing, insurance and credit [being able to borrow money] ... One of the most urgent tasks facing us in CARD therefore is to build a case by case exposure of discrimination, so that the Press and Parliament cannot pretend that it does not exist. If we are to campaign effectively against racial discrimination, we must publicise the evils which we are fighting.

From 'How to Expose Discrimination', a pamphlet produced by CARD (Campaign Against Racial Discrimination), which was formed in 1965.

1968: 'Rivers of Blood!'

Ten years after the Notting Hill riots came an equally controversial moment in the story of post-war immigration.

Despite government legislation, New Commonwealth immigration had continued to increase. It was changing too. Whereas immigration in the 1950s had been largely single people with no intention of staying in Britain, it was more commonly now people coming to settle, and in particular the wives and families of people already in Britain coming to join them. The biggest single non-white ethnic group were the Asians.

The arrival of the Kenyan Asians in 1967 had focused media and political attention on immigration once again. A far-right political party called the National Front was founded in 1967 and was dedicated to ending immigration and repatriating (sending home) all immigrants.

The National Front was an extremist party and it was easy to dismiss their views. However, it was less easy to ignore such views when they came from a respected and mainstream politician – enter Enoch Powell.

Powell was a former Cabinet member who had been tipped as a possible future Prime Minister. He was also Conservative MP for Wolverhampton, one of the centres of the Caribbean and Asian populations. Powell had been the Health Secretary in 1960 and had led the drive to recruit 18,000 Indian doctors, which effectively made the NHS possible.

Powell was a serious, respected and intelligent man. In April 1968, at a meeting of the Conservative Political Centre, he laid his career on the line. See what he had to say in Source 38, which contains extended extracts from his speech.

It was an explosive speech. For Powell, it ended his political career. He was sacked from the shadow cabinet and never returned. Yet 300 of the 412 Conservative constituency associations hailed Powell as a 'brave prophet'. In his own constituency of Wolverhampton 75 per cent said they agreed with what he had said. In London, dock workers stopped work and marched through London in support of him.

● **SOURCE 38**

(a) A week or two ago I fell into conversation with a constituent, a middle-aged, quite ordinary, working man employed in one of our nationalised industries. After a sentence or two about the weather, he suddenly said: 'If I had the money to go, I wouldn't stay in this country. I have three children, all of them been through grammar school and two of them married now, with family. I shan't be satisfied till I have seen them all settled overseas. In this country in 15 or 20 years' time the black man will have the whip hand over the white man.'

I can already hear the chorus of criticism. How dare I say such a horrible thing? How dare I stir up trouble and inflame feelings by repeating such a conversation? The answer is that I do not have the right not *to do so. Here is a decent, ordinary fellow Englishman, who in broad daylight in my own town says to me, his Member of Parliament, that his country will not be worth living in for his children.*

(b) In 15 or 20 years, on present trends, there will be in this country three and a half million Commonwealth immigrants and their descendants. That is not my figure. That is the official figure given to Parliament by the spokesman of the Registrar General's Office. Whole areas, towns and parts of towns across England will be occupied by sections of the immigrant and immigrant-descended population.

The natural and rational first question with a nation confronted by such a prospect is to ask: 'How can its dimensions be reduced?' The answers to the simple and rational question are equally simple and rational: by stopping, or virtually stopping, further inflow, and by promoting the maximum outflow.

(c) While, to the immigrant, entry to this country was admission to privileges and opportunities eagerly sought, the impact upon the existing population was very different. For reasons which they could not comprehend ... on which they were never consulted, they found themselves made strangers in their own country. They found their wives unable to obtain hospital beds in childbirth, their children unable to obtain school places, their homes and neighbourhoods changed beyond recognition, their plans and prospects for the future defeated; at work they found that employers hesitated to apply to the immigrant worker the standards of discipline and competence required of the native-born worker; they began to hear, as time went by, more and more voices which told them that they were now the unwanted.

The sense of being a persecuted minority which is growing among ordinary English people in the areas of the country which are affected is something that those without direct experience can hardly imagine.

(d) As I look ahead, I am filled with foreboding; like the Roman, I seem to see the River Tiber foaming with much blood.

Extracts from Enoch Powell's speech of 20 April 1968. The speech has become known as the 'Rivers of Blood speech'.

The Speech did just what Powell had hoped for the immigration debate – it caused a mighty stir. It galvanised opinion and action on either side.

● **SOURCE 39**

Pow! Wham! A cartoon by Leslie Illingworth that appeared in the *Daily Mail* on 24 April 1968.

● **SOURCE 40**

I dismissed Mr Powell because I believed his speech was inflammatory and liable to damage race relations ... I don't believe the great majority of the British people share Mr Powell's way of putting his views in his speech.

Edward Heath, leader of the Conservative Party, talking on *Panorama*, a BBC television programme, on 22 April 1968.

● **SOURCE 41**

A photograph published in the *London Evening Standard*, 1 May 1968.

● **SOURCE 42**

'You see, doc, I dropped my "I-back-Enoch" placard on my foot.'

A cartoon published in the *Daily Mail*, 24 April 1968.

Tasks

1 Study Source 38.
   a) What is Enoch Powell's main argument against immigration?
   b) What evidence is he using to back up his argument?
   c) What was the purpose of this speech?
2 Look at Sources 39–42. Which sources do you find most useful in assessing the reaction to Enoch Powell's speech?
3 Look at Source 42. How far do you trust this source as an accurate representation of reaction to Powell's speech?

How had immigrants contributed to British society by the early 1970s?

We first need to remind ourselves what kind of place Britain was in the 1940s. Six years of war had left the British government deep in debt, with cities damaged by wartime bombing and a depleted workforce decimated by wartime casualties. Despite the victory in war, the country was in many ways on its knees. The story of Britain's recovery from war is closely related to the story of post-war immigration.

The National Health Service

Without immigrant workers many public services simply could not have functioned. The National Health Service led the way in the 1940s. Thirty years later a vast number of the porters, cleaners, nurses, doctors, surgeons and consultants in the National Health Service were either immigrants or had immigrant roots.

● **SOURCE 43**

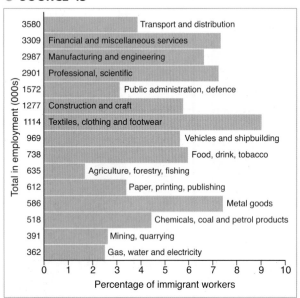

The percentage of immigrant workers in different sectors of the economy as revealed by the census in 1971.

Industry

Many industries were saved by immigrant workers. In Bradford, for example, textile mills were in trouble because the cost of making cloth was more than they could sell it for. The arrival of a large number of immigrants, mainly from Pakistan, who were prepared to work hard for low wages (by British standards) saved many of these mills. According to the 1971 census, over 100,000 workers were employed in the textiles and clothing industry (see Source 43). Even more were in engineering, largely in the West Midlands.

The inner cities

Immigrants went to live in some of the most rundown and damaged areas of Britain's inner cities and in the process they regenerated those areas. They (literally) rebuilt many homes. They also kept the areas alive in other ways: the Asian corner shop became a feature of almost all large towns and cities. By the 1960s many local stores were closing down because of competition from department stores and supermarkets. Asian entrepreneurs revived this type of business, providing local communities – black, Asian and white – with a much needed service, as well as making successful businesses. In Dewsbury, West Yorkshire, in the late 1960s all 37 off-licences were owned by Asian families.

Public transport

The buses and trains in London and in other cities depended very heavily on immigrant workers.

Culture

The ethnic immigrant population of Britain had risen from 100,000 in 1951 to 1,200,000 by 1971, yet that still represented only two per cent of the population.

If you lived outside of the large cities or the textile towns of Yorkshire and Lancashire, it is likely that you would never meet any one with a differently coloured skin.

However, in urban areas, post-war immigration had already had a significant impact on British culture. If you had been walking along the street in an English city in 1975 you would have seen, heard, touched and even tasted the influence of immigration.

Food

- Italian immigrants had introduced coffee bars and ice cream parlours to Britain.

- Immigrants from Cyprus had brought the taverna and the kebab.
- An astonishing 90 per cent of immigrants from Hong Kong had gone into the restaurant trade. By 1975 there was hardly a town or village in the United Kingdom without a Chinese takeaway or restaurant.
- There were almost 2,000 Indian restaurants in Britain by 1976. The immigrants showed their business sense by adapting their cuisine to British tastes. For example, you won't find Britain's favourite dish, chicken tikka masala, in India – it was created for the British because they liked gravy!

Music

- From the early calypso sounds that were brought to Britain by singers such as 'Lord Kitchener' on the SS *Empire Windrush* (see page 81), to the reggae sounds of Bob Marley and the Wailers in the 1970s, West Indian music became part of the British music scene.
- The Notting Hill Carnival introduced Britain to carnival: in the parade every August Bank Holiday floats, steel drum bands and sound systems blasted out the latest sounds of the Caribbean across West London.
- One of the most successful British and international rock bands of the 1970s, Queen, was fronted by Farrokh Bulsara who was born in Zanzibar and educated in Bombay (and who changed his name to Freddie Mercury).

Religion

- Immigrants from India and Pakistan brought Hindu and Muslim religions to the heart of British communities.
- Immigrants from the Caribbean revitalised Christianity in British cities. It was a time when many in the white community were losing faith and churches were closing. Many were kept open by the influx of Christians from the Caribbean and their characteristic music – gospel – was spreading out into the mainstream music industry.
- Former churches in Britain's cities were converted into mosques, gurdwaras and temples as well as Pentecostal churches.

Popular culture

- Trinidadian journalist Trevor Macdonald became the first black newsreader in 1973.
- By the end of the 1970s black players had begun to break through into top flight professional football. The so-called 'Three Degrees' (Laurie Cunningham, Cyrille Regis and Brendan Batson) played football for West Bromwich Albion – despite facing monkey chants from the terraces and having bananas thrown at them.
- Popular television sitcoms *'Til Death Us Do Part* and *Love Thy Neighbour* focused on attitudes to race and immigration.

Individuals

Sybil Phoenix, MBE

Sybil Phoenix arrived in Britain from Guyana in 1956. Her first room was in a leaking basement in London. (She cooked her first Christmas dinner in Britain under an umbrella!) As an orphan herself she was determined to help other orphans. She became a foster parent and gave a home to over 100 children. She opened a youth club called the Moonshot in Lewisham and helped to found the early race relations groups in the area. Even when arsonists burnt down her youth club, she did not give up her work. In 1971 Phoenix was awarded an MBE (Member of the (Order of the) British Empire) and in 1973 became mayoress of Lewisham.

Sir Anwar Pervez

Anwar Pervez came from a farming family in Pakistan in 1956. He drove buses in Bradford before opening a convenience store in Earls Court, London, in 1962. This grew into the Bestway chain with stores all over the country. Pervez became very wealthy. His Bestway Foundation helps to fund schools in needy areas. He was knighted in 1999.

These are two big names. Millions of other ordinary immigrants of the post-war period were welcomed by some and rejected by others. Many had to overcome prejudice and discrimination in the workplace and on the streets. Some chose to ignore it and carry on as best as they could, while others chose to fight back. Either way, they settled into communities across the length and breadth of Britain and became part of the make-up of the country.

What was the situation by 1975?

The period covered by this Depth Study is 1939–1975. If you had asked for an ordinary Briton's view on the state of their country in 1975, they would probably have given quite a depressing summary.

In the 1970s Britain entered a major economic crisis. Unemployment soared. Inflation soared. There were strikes in almost all major industries. The government debt grew so much that Britain needed bailing out by the International Monetary Fund (IMF). At one stage the government ordered all industries to reduce to a three-day working week to conserve energy supplies, which had been hit by strikes. It was a very unsettled time.

What's more, it was also a time of increasing racial tension. With massive unemployment Britain no longer needed any more workers. Some people saw immigration as part of the problem rather than part of the solution to Britain's economic problems.

There remained those who still shared the fears of Enoch Powell. In 1972 Leicester City Council for example warned that 'the entire fabric of our city is at risk' because the immigrant population was beginning to outnumber the white population. (However, note that just ten years later the city was still standing and indeed had begun a festival of cultures to celebrate the different peoples in it.)

The right wing, anti-immigration party, the National Front, was gaining supporters. In Leicester it gained 18 per cent of the vote in a local election.

Day-to-day discrimination

The ideal of 'equal opportunity' was not fully achieved by the 1970s. Laws had made discrimination in housing and employment illegal but they were often hard to enforce. Discrimination continued in more subtle ways: for example, schools tended to have lower expectations of black and Asian students so these students had lower expectations of themselves and thus gained fewer qualifications. Black and Asian communities faced higher unemployment rates than the UK average and those in work found it hard to get promoted.

Racial violence

In an echo of the 1958 Notting Hill riots, the latest version of youth gangs – the skinheads – became infamous for 'Paki-bashing'. The particular focus of this was the Asian communities in the London areas of Bethnal Green, Newham and Southall. Girls were kicked on their way to school, stones were thrown at windows, and eggs and tomatoes were hurled at families who dared step outside. Following a murder in 1976, the leader of the National Front said in public 'one down, a million to go'.

● **SOURCE 44**

'No, we're not police—we're psychiatrists.'

A cartoon from the *Daily Mail*, 16 January 1974.

Task

1   Study Source 44. Why was this source published in 1974?

Tasks

2   It is very hard (and quite dangerous) to generalise about the experiences of immigrants. Every person is an individual with their own story. However historians still try.
    a)   Which three sources or pieces of information would you choose for an 'evidence file' to show how awful life was for immigrants to Britain in the period 1950–1975?
    b)   Which three sources or pieces of information would you choose for an 'evidence file' to show that life was good for immigrants in the period 1950–1975?
    You do not need to limit yourself to pages 58–73. You can research your own sources from elsewhere. Write a paragraph to explain your files.
3   If you put your two files together, do you think they make an accurate picture of the experiences of immigrants?
4   What does compiling your files teach you about handling evidence on immigration?

Key points

What contribution had immigrants made to British society by the early 1970s?

• Immigrants formed much of the workforce in public service such as transport and the NHS.
• Immigrants had broadened British music and diet, and had begun to change the culture of British cities.

Did the National Health Service help or hinder women?

The large numbers of civilian casualties during the Second World War led to the government becoming more involved in medical care. Gradually the idea developed that this involvement should continue after the war. In 1942 a leading civil servant, William Beveridge, put forward the idea that there should be a National Health Service that would provide medical care for every man, woman and child in the country. The important thing about this new service was that it would be free.

In 1945 a new Labour government was elected, and the following year a bill to introduce the NHS was passed by parliament. On 5 July 1948 the new National Health Service swung into operation. It was intended to make life easier for everyone by taking some of the worry and strain away from being ill or having a family member in need of medical help. But did it? Did the NHS, in reality, make life easier or more difficult for women?

Read all the sources, then answer the questions on page 77.

● **SOURCE A**

"Dentist says if there are any more of you thinking of fitting one another up with National Health teeth for Christmas presents you've had it."

A cartoon published in the *Daily Express* newspaper, 1949.

● **SOURCE B**

I was an apprentice in 1948. I spent some time at the School of Pharmacy and some at the chemist's shop. When I came in to the shop on the first day of the National Health Service, there were fifty prescriptions. In those days that was amazing. Before then the highest ever had been about twenty. People seemed to go mad. I knew lots of people who got two sets of false teeth. Why did you need two sets one day when you had none the day before? I heard stories about people taking sheets of surgical gauze and using them as net curtains!

Frank Walsh, a Liverpool pharmacist, describes the early days of the NHS.

● SOURCE C

My mother used to sit in a misery of embarrassment on the edge of a chair in the consulting room on the rare and desperate days when one of us had to be taken to the doctor – opening and shutting her purse, waiting for the right moment to extract the careful, unspareable, half crown. She never knew whether just to slide it across the desk, which she said might make the doctor feel like a waiter, or to actually put it in his hand and make him feel as if he worked in a shop. Sometimes we dropped the money and that was the least dignified of all, especially if the fat doctor let my mother pick it up. And sometimes he would shout at my mother for not having come before, like the time we had to wait for my sister's sore throat to turn unmistakably into diphtheria before she was pushed off in a pram to his surgery. 'Good God, woman, why didn't you bring this child days ago?'

A newspaper article published in 1964, in which the writer remembers healthcare in the 1930s.

● SOURCE D

Medical treatment should be made available to rich and poor alike in accordance with medical need and no other criteria. Worry about money in a time of sickness is a serious hindrance to recovery, apart from its unnecessary cruelty. The records show that it is the mother in the average family who suffers most from the absence of a full health service. In trying to balance her budget, she puts her own needs last. No society can call itself civilised if a sick person is denied medical aid because of lack of means. The essence of a satisfactory health service is that the rich and poor are treated alike, that poverty is not a disability and wealth is not advantaged.

Aneurin (Nye) Bevan, Minister of Health, in a speech in 1946.

● SOURCE E

The whole time I was pregnant with Mandy, I felt uneasy. For some reason I had a feeling that the baby might have Down's Syndrome but my mother told me not to be silly.

In those days – the early sixties – there wasn't much you could do about it, anyway. There were no scans to pick up abnormalities and certainly no question of termination.

I took the drug Thalidomide regularly during the pregnancy. My GP prescribed it on the NHS, not for morning sickness, but as a sedative because I was having trouble sleeping. We didn't ask questions in those days, we just did exactly what our doctors told us to do. Towards the end of my pregnancy the GP told me to stop taking the drug, as there might be problems with it. But we didn't know what.

I went into natural labour and Mandy was born quickly. The doctors took her from me before I could even see her. I was terrified. Then a doctor came to tell me her arms were badly deformed and they wouldn't allow me to see her until my husband Len arrived.

The nurses brought this little baby in to us and she was beautiful. The fact that she had no arms didn't bother us. After all that fuss we were just relieved she was alive and healthy.

We brought Mandy home and, lying her on the floor, unwrapped all her clothes so that her four brothers and sisters could take a good look. From that moment on they just accepted her as one of them.

June Hornsby describes what it was like in 1962 when her daughter Mandy was born without arms because her NHS doctor had prescribed thalidomide while she was pregnant. From an article in the *Mail Online* in July 2008.

SOURCE F

An anti-smoking poster produced by the government's Health Education Council in the 1960s.

SOURCE G

You could get the Pill on the NHS and easy abortion on the NHS. So it was very difficult to say 'No' to a boy who wanted to sleep with you. Sure, there was no fear of having an unwanted baby, but that fear was replaced by a whole lot of other decisions that could end up with you being labelled 'frigid' or 'an easy lay' by the gang you went around with. More girls' reputations were ruined than ever before.

Ann Walsh remembers growing up in the 1970s.

SOURCE H

A photograph of young women running a petition in support of their defeat of the abortion amendment bill and campaign in defence of women's right to abortion.

Questions

1   Study **Source A**.
    What point is the cartoonist making about the National Health Service?
    Use the source in your answer. [5]

2   Study **Sources A** and **B**.
    How far does Source B agree with Source A about the early days of the National Health Service?
    Use the sources and your own knowledge in your answer. [6]

3   Study **Sources C** and **D**.
    How likely do you think it would be that women, in particular, would benefit from the new National Health Service?
    Use the sources and your own knowledge in your answer. [7]

4   Study **Sources D** and **E**.
    'Source E proves that the National Health Service didn't help mothers.'
    Do you agree with this statement? Use the sources and your own knowledge to explain your answer. [8]

5   Study **Source F**.
    How useful is this source to a historian trying to find out how the National Health Service tried to keep young people healthy?
    Use the source and your own knowledge in your answer. [6]

6   Study **Sources G** and **H**.
    How far does Source H challenge the views expressed in Source G?
    Use the sources and your own knowledge in your answer. [8]

7   Study **all** the sources and use your own knowledge.
    'The National Health Service hindered, rather than helped, women.'
    Explain whether or not you agree with this view. [10]

How to tackle the conclusion question

The final question in a source investigation can look quite daunting.

It is worth most marks and you should spend the most time on it. Here is what to do:

1   Do you agree with the statement? The examiner wants you to make your mind up and use your knowledge **and** the sources to support your viewpoint.

    However, make sure you consider both sides of the statement. Even if you agree with it, make sure you consider the evidence that contradicts it too.

2   Write at least two paragraphs: one to cover the evidence against, the other looking at the evidence to support it. Then write a concluding paragraph. Your concluding paragraph should sum up your overall view. This is also the best place to make points about the reliability of sources.

3   You don't need to mention every source in your answer. Just focus on one or two sources on each side – the strongest evidence.

4   Include details or quotes from the sources in your answer.

5   You should refer to a source by authorship or content not by letter. Don't write 'As Source B says ...', write 'As the pharmacist recalls in Source B ...'.

Back to home and duty?

Read all the sources, then answer the questions on page 80.

During the Second World War (1939–45) women formed a vital part of the workforce. They were needed to keep the country going: to work in industry, transport and agriculture in order to support the armed forces overseas and to fill the gaps left by the men who had been called up to fight. However, once the war was over and the men returned, what happened to the women? Were they expected to go back to being wives and mothers? Was all that had been gained during the war now lost?

● **SOURCE A**

Dame Laura Knight was an official war artist, appointed by the government to paint wartime scenes. In 1943, she painted this picture of Ruby Loftus working in a secret gun-making factory in Newport, South Wales. Ruby was a lathe operator, one of a handful of women who were able to perform such highly skilled work. Before the war she had worked as a shop assistant.

● **SOURCE B**

Princess Elizabeth, who became Queen Elizabeth II in 1953, joined the Auxiliary Territorial Service in 1945. This was against the wishes of the British government and her parents, who were then King and Queen.

● **SOURCE C**

Soon, many women took up the idea that if they were doing men's jobs, then they should get men's pay. Equal pay for women workers became a key debate that occupied the unions during the war and which led to several strikes, most famously at Hillington Rolls-Royce plant near Glasgow in 1943. When the workforce rejected an initial settlement to their pay claim, 16,000 women and men walked out. Initially, other local workers joined the strike despite the fact that the local and national press had labelled the strikers 'traitors'. Eventually a settlement was reached whereby a rate was fixed for every machine in the factory, regardless of the sex of the operator.

From *The Women's Army* by Judith Orr, published in March 1995.

● **SOURCE D**

This cartoon was published in March 1954.

● **SOURCE E**

Day-to-Day Plan for New Brides

Monday Clean the kitchen after week-end catering activities, check up on rations and shop for vegetables, canned food and breakfast cereals for a few days ahead.

Tuesday Wash personal laundry, leaving the sheets and bath towels. Get all items dried and ironed during the day whenever possible.

Wednesday Clean bedrooms and bathrooms thoroughly and use the early afternoon for cleaning the silver.

Thursday Change bed linen, wash sheets, pillowcases and towels. While they dry, clean the lounge. Iron in the afternoon.

Friday Plan meals for the weekend, remembering to have left-overs for Monday. Shop. Give the dining room a thorough clean and polish.

Saturday Keep this free for the family as far as possible. Prepare vegetables for Sunday and manage some cooking in the morning. Relax.

Sunday Belongs to you and those who share the home with you. Confine all essential cooking to the early part of the morning.

What you wear in the house for the working hours is important. Crisp easily removed, cheerful overalls, smocks, nylon or spongeable plastic aprons look attractive. Wear your hair as you would do for the man-of-the-house's homecoming.

From a brochure issued in 1947 by the furniture-makers James Broderick & Co., and used by thousands of housewives in the 1950s.

● **SOURCE F**

Taken as a whole, the plan for social security puts a very high importance on marriage. In the next thirty years, housewives as mothers have vital work to do in ensuring the continuance of the British race and British ideals in the world.

From Sir William Beveridge's report, which laid down the foundations of the welfare state, published in 1942.

● **SOURCE G**

I scanned through Bowlby [John Bowlby's book 'Child Care and the Growth of Love'] to see if it was all right to go out for half an hour and certainly, below the age of three, you were not really meant to leave the child at all. I had some of those feelings they call being depersonalised. I didn't know who I was any more and I didn't find myself enjoying anything very much. It was more a sort of endurance test getting through that time. I knew that the minute she went to proper school, it would be OK to go out to work and that is exactly what I did.

Berry Myall, who had her first baby in the 1950s shortly after graduating from Cambridge University, explains how she felt about having to stay at home with her daughter.

Questions

1   Study **Source A**.
    What can you learn from this source about the government's attitude to women workers?
    Use the source in your answer.   [6]

2   Study **Sources A** and **B**.
    Which source would be the more useful to a historian trying to find out about the work that women did in the Second World War?
    Use the sources and your own knowledge in your answer.   [8]

3   Study **Sources C** and **D**.
    How far does Source D challenge what Source C says about equal pay for women workers?
    Use the sources and your own knowledge in your answer.   [9]

4   Study **Source E**.
    Does Source E prove that all women returned to being housewives after the war?
    Use the source and your own knowledge in your answer.   [8]

5   Study **Sources F** and **G**.
    Does Source F explain what was happening in Source G?   [7]

6   Use **all** the sources and your own knowledge.
    'Everything gained by women during the Second World War was lost in the 1950s.'
    How far would you agree with this statement?   [12]

Great Britain: land of opportunity for Caribbean immigrants?

Read all the sources, then answer the questions on page 83.

By 1965, about a quarter of a million Caribbean immigrants were living in Great Britain. They had come with high hopes of a better life and higher living standards. But how realistic were these expectations? Was Great Britain really the land of opportunity they had hoped for?

● **SOURCE A**

What next? A cartoon by Sid Moon that appeared in the *Sunday Dispatch*, 28 February 1948.

● **SOURCE B**

London is the place for me,
London this lovely city,
To live in London you are really comfortable,
Because the English people are very much sociable,
They take you here and they take you there,
And they make you feel like a millionaire,
London that's the place for me.

A song written by 'Lord Kitchener' (real name Aldwyn Roberts),
who arrived in Britain on the SS *Empire Windrush* in 1948.

● SOURCE C

(1) Port of Embarkation	(2) Port at which Passengers have been landed	(3) NAMES OF PASSENGERS		(4) CLASS (Whether 1st, 2nd, Tourist or 3rd)	(5) AGES OF PASSENGERS							(6) Proposed Address in the United Kingdom	(7) Profession, Occupation, or Calling of Passengers	(8) Country of last Permanent Residence*	(9) Country of Intended Future Permanent Residence*					
					Adults of 19 years and upwards				Children between 1 and 12		Infants				England	Wales	Scotland	Northern Ireland	Eire	Other parts of the British Empire	Foreign Countries
					Accompanied by husband or wife		Not Accompanied by husband or wife													
					Males	Females	Males	Females	Males	Females	Males	Females									
24. TRINIDAD.	Tilbury	DUGDALE	Joseph	"A"	29								Broxup,Bolton-by- Bowland,Nr.Clitheroe.	Planter.	Trinidad.						●	
25. "	"	"	Stella	"		31							-do-	H.D.	"						●	
26. "	"	EGNOLU	John	"			32						c/o Dir.of Col.Scholars, Colonial Office.W.1.	Student.	"							●
27. "	"	FORBES	Mary	"				41					St.Catherines Torres, Morayshire Hill Gdns.	H.D.	British Guiana.		●					
28. "	"	FRASER	Muriel	"				39					Twickenham,Middlx.	Bank Clerk.	"							●
29. "	"	GANDY	Adelaide	"				47					Hillingdon,Farnbridge Park,Hants.	H.D.	England.	●						
30. "	"	GRANT	Flora	"		59							41.Hardgate,Aberdeen.	"	Trinidad.							●
31. "	"	"	Lewis	"A"	58								-do-	Merchant.	"							●
32. "	"	GALLEY	Wilfred	"		25							35.Hartburn Lane, Stockton-on-Tees.	Agriculturalist.	Uganda.						●	
33. "	"	HARRIS	Grace	"				45					Laudton House. Launton.Oxon.	H.D.	England.	●						
34. "	"	HICKSON	Audrey	"				30					c/o Lloyds Bank. 16.St.James'St.S.W.1.	Master Mariner.	St.Lucia.						●	
35. "	"	HOOD	Hugh	"			39	39					Gourock.		Trinidad.						●	
36. "	"	HERON	Margaret	"				64					116.Queens Gate.S.W.7. 7.Clarence Gate Gdns.	H.D.							●	
37. "	"	HORAY	Ivy	"				51					London.N.W.1.	Civil	England.	●						
38. "	"	HAMEL-SMITH	Eric	"			36						96.High St.S.W.6. Rutford House.	Servant.	Trinidad.						●	
39. "	"	JONES	Alfred	"			37						Rutford Place.W.1									

Part of a page from the passenger list of SS *Empire Windrush*, which sailed on 24 May 1948 for Tilbury Docks in England.

● SOURCE D

This photo was used as part of the recruitment campaign by London Transport to attract workers from the Caribbean.

● SOURCE E

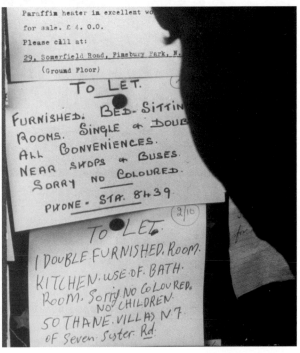

A young Jamaican immigrant looking for accommodation in the late 1950s.

SI 3 GREAT BRITAIN: LAND OF OPPORTUNITY FOR CARIBBEAN IMMIGRANTS?

● SOURCE F

NEW DANCE HALL: OWNERS TO BAN COLOURED FOLK

The doors of a new dance hall in Wolverhampton are soon to be opened to the dancing public. But the sign is to go up: 'No coloured dancers' – neither will 'Teddy Boys' be admitted.

The manager said the ban will be enforced for 'business reasons'. He added there always seemed to be troubles of some kind when coloured dancers were admitted. Then he stated: 'If it warrants it they can have their own night for dancing.'

From the *Wolverhampton Express and Star*, 6 February 1955.

● SOURCE G

Jamaicans' friend leaving Wolverhampton

Wolverhampton Methodists can be proud of the Rev Howard Belben [who is moving to Sheffield]. He takes the trouble to visit the homes of West Indian and other coloured worshippers and runs a monthly 'international fellowship', a kind of social-cum-prayer meeting. And he somehow manages to remember all [about 300] of his West Indians' names (a fact which endears him to them).

An extract from the *Wolverhampton Express and Star*, 1957.

Questions

1   Study **Source A**.
    What can you learn from this source about the cartoonist's attitude to immigration?
    Use the source in your answer.   [6]

2   Study **Source C**.
    One of the arguments made in parliament was that passengers from the *Windrush* were going to help rebuild Britain.
    How far does this source support that argument?
    Use the source and your own knowledge in your answer.   [8]

3   Study **Sources B** and **D**.
    How reliable are these sources as evidence about opportunities for immigrants in Britain?
    Use the sources and your own knowledge in your answer.   [7]

4   Study **Sources D** and **E**.
    Does Source E challenge Source D about life in Britain for immigrants?
    Use the sources and your own knowledge in your answer.   [8]

5   Study **Sources F** and **G**.
    How far do these sources prove that a colour bar was developing in Britain?
    Use the sources and your own knowledge in your answer.   [9]

6   Study **all** the sources and your own knowledge.
    'Great Britain was a land of opportunity for Caribbean immigrants.'
    How far would you agree with this statement?   [12]

Was the Sex Discrimination Act of 1975 really necessary?

In 1975, parliament passed the Sex Discrimination Act. Its aim was to protect both men and women from discrimination on the grounds of sex. It applied mainly to employment, training, education, harassment and the provision of goods and services. But was it really necessary?

Read all the sources, then answer the questions on page 86.

● **SOURCE A**

"This is what comes of marrying a career woman."

A cartoon published in the magazine *Punch* in the 1950s.

● **SOURCE B**

Ask any man if he'd rather his wife worked or stayed at home and see what he says; he would rather she stayed at home and looked after his children, and was waiting for him with a decent meal and a sympathetic ear when he got home from work. You can't have deep and safe happiness in marriage and the exciting independence of a career as well.

Monica Dickens, an author, in the magazine *Woman's Own*, 28 January 1961.

● **SOURCE C**

I left my all-girls grammar school in 1964. The teachers encouraged us to believe that we could follow any career we wanted: electrical engineering, architecture, law, and business – it didn't matter. All we had to do was work hard, get a good degree and the world was ours. Then we had a talk by a Miss Petty from the county careers office. She outlined everything we could do and was very enthusiastic when one of my friends said she wanted to be a social anthropologist. But Miss Petty ended her talk by saying that the best careers for women were teaching and nursing because they fitted in so well with family life. I bet she didn't tell the boys that!

Rosemary Dawson remembers the careers advice she was given in the 1960s.

SI 4 WAS THE SEX DISCRIMINATION ACT OF 1975 REALLY NECESSARY?

● SOURCE D

Something had to be done about the fact that women were earning about 70 per cent of what men were being paid for the same work. More significantly, something had to be done about the fact that very few women reached any kind of seniority within factories, that men were always the bosses and women always subservient. And so some of us became involved in a campaign to get equal pay for women. In 1970, just as we were about to go to university, the Equal Pay Act became law, and we thought that the issue which of all issues most concerned us, had been won. We should have known better. Men did not suddenly decide that they had been monstrously unfair to women, nor did the trades unions show any serious interest in fighting for women's rights.

From *Whatever's Happening to Women* by Julia Neuberger, published in 1991. Julia Neuberger was a student at Cambridge University in 1970 when the Women's Liberation Movement took a hold in England. She is now a rabbi, wife, mother, broadcaster and writer.

● SOURCE E

After the Equal Pay Act I visited a shoe factory where they were making men's shoes and women's shoes. There were a lot of women putting heels on shoes. And there were a lot of men in another part of the factory putting heels on shoes. I said to the manager, 'I suppose you have equal pay?' And he said, 'Oh yes, we have equal pay.' So I asked him, 'Do you mean to say that the women here running this machine and the men over there running the same machine, get the same pay?' He said, 'Oh no, heavens no! Those men are putting heels on men's shoes. The women are putting heels on women's shoes. It's not the same work.' There were six nails going into each shoe and they were using the same machines. But the women didn't get the same pay.

Hazel Hunkins-Hallinan, a campaigner for women's rights, describes a visit she made to a shoe factory after the Equal Pay Act of 1970.

● SOURCE F

TEACHING A GIRL ABOUT HERTZ
IS TEACHING HER TO SAY YES

Before every new Hertz girl meets her public, she has to learn to always say Yes to a customer.

It's easy when you work for Hertz because there's no limit to what Hertz has to offer. In fact, it takes us six weeks to fill her pretty head with all the facts and figures.

What we don't spell out is what we know a Hertz girl can handle naturally. We choose her because she's the kind of girl who enjoys solving all the little things that don't seem little at the time.

Yes, I'll phone your wife to tell her you'll be late.

Yes, I'll find the briefcase you left in the car.

Yes, I'll sew the button on your coat.

The next time you want to rent a car, ask a Hertz girl. You'll see how well she has learned her lessons.

An advertisement published in *The Times*, 12 October 1972. Hertz was, and still is, a company that deals in rental cars.

● **SOURCE G**

I was thirty-three and full of vim and vigour. I wanted to change the world. In 1972 most of the book publishing companies were run by men and most of the books I wanted to read were not published by them. Starting Virago was not difficult, except in obvious ways – there was no money. The banks were unfriendly and pompous. That was usual. In those days single women couldn't get a mortgage, either.

In the early days I spent a lot of time explaining to journalists that I did not hate men. I simply wanted women's history, lives and literature to be placed in printed form alongside men's published experience of the same. I suppose my greatest achievement while I was there was to lay down standards for excellence and competence, and in doing so, to make it possible for other women in business to do well.

From an article by Carmen Callil, published in the *Sunday Telegraph* in June 1993. Carmen Callil founded the women's publishing company Virago in 1972. It was highly successful.

● **SOURCE H**

At the end of the sixties, women were involved in all major social trends of the period, from the increasingly flexible nature of work and the technological transformation of the household to the liberalisation of divorce and the legislation of abortion. By having smaller families, expanding into the workforce and asserting their equal status with men, women participated in British national life as never before.

From *White Heat: A History of Britain in the Swinging Sixties* by Dominic Sandbrook, published in 2006.

Questions

1 Study **Source A.**
What point is the cartoonist making about working women?
Use the source in your answer. [5]

2 Study **Sources B** and **C.**
Which of these sources is the more useful to a historian enquiring into opportunities for women in the 1960s?
Use the sources and your own knowledge in your answer. [7]

3 Study **Sources D** and **E.**
How far do these two sources prove that the Equal Pay Act of 1970 didn't help end discrimination against women?
Use the sources and your own knowledge in your answer. [8]

4 Study **Source F.**
Are you surprised that an advertisement like this could appear in 1972?
Use the source and your own knowledge in your answer. [9]

5 Study **Sources G** and **H.**
How far does Source G support Source H in what it says about women's participation in British national life?
Use the sources and your own knowledge in your answer. [9]

6 Study **all** the sources and use your own knowledge.
'The Sex Discrimination Act of 1975 was completely unnecessary.'
Explain whether or not you agree with this view. [12]

Did everyone benefit from the prosperity of the 1950s?

In July 1957 the Prime Minister, Harold Macmillan, said that most people in Britain had 'never had it so good'. After the economic problems of the 1930s and the suffering and sacrifices of the war years, an economic upturn in the world economy meant that British products were selling well around the world. Britain had full employment – everyone who was able to work could get a job: including teenagers when they left school. This growing prosperity (people being well off) is seen by many historians as creating the first teenage 'youth culture': when teens had enough money and free time to do their own thing instead of just acting like their parents. But did this change affect everyone in the same way? Did everyone growing up in the 1950s benefit from this prosperity?

Read all the sources, then answer the questions on page 90.

● **SOURCE A**

A cartoon published in the *New Statesman* on Boxing Day, 1959. The TV screen reads 'I'm All Right Jack', which means something like: 'I'm busy looking after myself and I don't have any time for you'. It was also the title of a hit British film in 1959. Note the Christian symbols of Christmas – the star and the stable.

● SOURCE B

Possibly the most novel finding [of this report] is the extent of poverty among children. For over a decade it has been generally assumed that such poverty as exists is found overwhelmingly among the aged [the elderly] ... We have estimated that there were about two and a quarter million children in low income households in 1960. Thus qualitatively the problem of poverty among children is more than two-thirds of the size of poverty among the aged. This fact has not been given due emphasis in the policies of the political parties. It is also worth observing that there were substantially more children in poverty than adults of working age ... On the whole the data we have presented contradicts the commonly held view that a trend towards greater equality has accompanied the trend towards greater affluence.

From Brian Abel-Smith and Peter Townsend, *The Poor and the Poorest*, published in 1965.

● SOURCE C

A poster advertising holidays in North Yorkshire in 1953.

● SOURCE D

A family watching television in the 1950s. Do you think this is a very well-off family or quite an ordinary family?

SI 5 DID EVERYONE BENEFIT FROM THE PROSPERITY OF THE 1950S?

● **SOURCE E**

... increased earnings come from the increasing production of most of our main industries – steel, coal, motor cars; a large part of the increase is going to exports or to investment. That is all to the good. Indeed, let us be frank about it: most of our people have never had it so good. Go around the country, go to the industrial towns, go to the farms, and you will see a state of prosperity such as we have never had in my lifetime – nor indeed ever in the history of this country.

What is beginning to worry some of us is, is it too good to be true? – or perhaps I should say, is it too good to last?

Harold Macmillan's speech at Bedford, 20 July 1957 (reported in *The Times*, 22 July 1957). Although you'll often read about the phrase 'never had it so good' in books and websites on the 1950s, notice that Macmillan's overall message is quite cautious.

● **SOURCE F**

First a young mother [said to the 1950s survey]: 'Dad used to be very strict with us, we are different with our boy. We make more of a mate of him. When I was a kid Dad always had the best of everything. Now it's the children who get the best of it. If there's one pork chop left, the kiddie gets it'; and a young father: 'There's certainly been a change. I whack mine now, but not the beatings we used to have. When I was a boy most of us feared our fathers more than we liked them. I know I feared mine and I had plenty of reason to.'

From *The Penguin Social History of Britain: British Society Since 1945* by Arthur Marwick, published in 1996.

● **SOURCE G**

In 1960 the last call-up papers were sent out to just over 2000 young men. Until the 1960s every young man who left school knew that he would have to go into one of the three services, probably the army, and by the time National Service was finished, 5.3 million teenagers would have learned to stand straight with their shoulders back. Their hair would have been cut in the 'short back and sides' style. They would have learned to look after themselves, probably for the first time having to do their own laundry, washing and scrubbing three times a day ... When they returned from National Service the opportunity to make their own way from teenage to adulthood had been taken away. In the 1960s the first teenagers since 1938 crossed into adult life at their own pace and in their own style.

From *This Sceptred Isle: Twentieth Century* by Christopher Lee, published in 1999.

PART 3 SOURCE INVESTIGATIONS

● **SOURCE H**

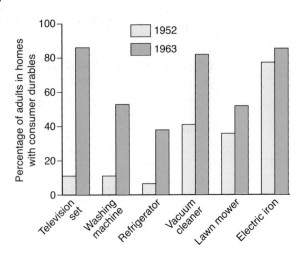

From *Britain in the Twentieth Century: A Documentary Reader Volume II: 1939–1970*, edited by Lawrence Butler and Harriet Jones, published in 1995.

Questions

1 Study **Source A**.
What is the main point the cartoonist is making about the new prosperity of the 1950s?
Use the source in your answer. [5]

2 Study **Sources A** and **B**.
How far does Source B agree with Source A in its message about whether everyone – including children – 'never had it so good'?
Use the sources and your own knowledge in your answer. [6]

3 Study **Sources C** and **D**.
How would having a TV and being able to go on holidays have made a difference to children's lives in the 1950s?
Use the sources and your own knowledge in your answer. [7]

4 Study **Source E**.
'Source E proves that Britain was enjoying unprecedented prosperity by the late 1950s.'
Do you agree? Use the source and your own knowledge to explain your answer. [8]

5 Study **Sources F** and **G**.
Many commentators were concerned that young people were being treated too softly in the 1950s. How far do Sources G and F challenge or support this view?
Use the sources and your own knowledge in your answer. [8]

6 Study **Source H**.
How useful is this source to a historian trying to find out how far everyone growing up in the 1950s benefited from prosperity?
Use the source and your own knowledge in your answer. [6]

7 Study **all** the sources and use your own knowledge.
'Most people in the 1950s had "never had it so good".'
Explain whether or not you agree with this view. [10]

Why did young people in Britain get political in the 1960s?

One of the big changes in the way young people behaved in the 1960s was to do with politics. Many young people felt very strongly about political issues such as free speech, civil rights, the rights of women and, most famously, America's war in Vietnam. Many British students agreed with American student protestors that the war was completely wrong: the USA was bombing helpless Vietnamese people in a bloodthirsty campaign against communist North Vietnam. However, no British students were in danger of being sent to Vietnam, British students could not vote in US elections and most British people viewed Vietnam as somebody else's war, a long way away. So why did British young people get so passionately involved with anti-Vietnam protests and what does that say about changes in the way young people behaved in the 1960s and early 1970s?

Read all the sources, then answer the questions on page 93.

● **SOURCE A**

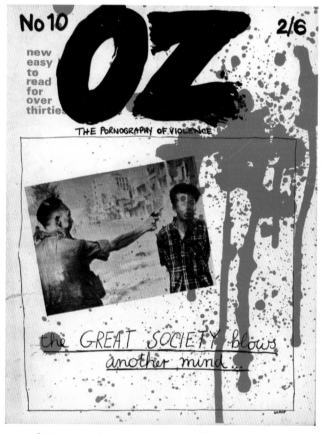

This is the cover of *Oz* magazine from March 1968. *Oz* was a satirical underground magazine and was very popular with students who wanted to rebel against the values of mainstream society. This cover includes a famous photo of a South Vietnamese police chief executing a Vietcong fighter. The 'Great Society' was US President Johnson's project for improving life for all in the USA, so the line on the cover – 'Great Society blows another mind' – is saying the USA was responsible for this killing.

● SOURCE B

There was ... the relentlessness of the bombing ... and I put a map of Vietnam on my wall. I think people now probably don't understand that, but it was just terrible. Everything that was progress was being used to destroy. Every day you opened the paper there were unknown tonnages [of bombs] going thousands of miles to pulverise peasants.

Anthony Barnett, a student at Leicester University in 1968, remembers how he felt about the Vietnam war, quoted in 'The Viet Nam War and the British Student Left: A Study in Political Symbolism' by Anthony O. Edmonds, published in 1994.

● SOURCE C

Politics never entered my head. There I was at school learning French, German, English and Latin, but I completely missed the Vietnam War. I didn't know it was on, frankly. I can only recall hearing about them pulling out, and thinking, pulling out of where?

Quoted in *The Seventies: Good Times, Bad Taste* by Alison Pressley, published in 2002.

● SOURCE D

'Don't take it too hard—there may be a breakdown.'

This cartoon by 'Trog' (Wally Fawkes) was first published by the *Daily Mail* on 17 May 1968. The Paris Peace Talks were designed to end the war in Vietnam. In fact there was a breakdown in the peace talks and the war continued until 1973.

● SOURCE E

Ev'rywhere I hear the sound of marching, charging feet, boy
'Cause summer's here and the time is right for fighting in the street, boy
But what can a poor boy do
Except to sing for a rock 'n' roll band
'Cause in sleepy London town
There's just no place for a street fighting man
No

First verse of 'Street Fighting Man' by The Rolling Stones, from the album *Beggars Banquet*, released on Decca Records in 1968. Mick Jagger wrote this song after going on the anti-Vietnam demonstration in Grosvenor Square. The song was banned by a number of UK radio stations.

● SOURCE F

British police blocking off Grosvenor Square (site of the American Embassy) in London as rioting breaks out during an anti-Vietnam war demonstration in March 1968.

● SOURCE G

Many people copied the style of American protest movements because they thought they were fashionable, and this explains why American practices, like calling authority figures 'pigs' and 'fascists', appeared in Britain in the late sixties. In the United States this kind of language reflected the genuine social tensions of the day and the fevered debate over the Vietnam War; in Britain, however, it sounded trite and incongruous. Sue Miles thought her contemporaries were 'all copying American culture', and admitted: 'We were not pushed by any major issues. There was no draft, you could piss around in England quite a lot'... The peace movement was never likely to attract mass support for the simple reason that most people simply did not care enough about a war in which they were not directly involved.

From *White Heat: A History of Britain in the Swinging Sixties* by Dominic Sandbrook, published in 2006.

Questions

1 Study **Source A**.
   What can you learn from this source about British students' attitudes to the Vietnam War?
   Use the source to explain your answer. [7]

2 Study **Sources A**, **B** and **C**.
   How useful are these sources to a historian studying student involvement in politics in the 1960s?
   Use the sources and your own knowledge to explain your answer. [9]

3 Study **Source D**.
   Is the cartoonist supporting or criticising student political protest?
   Use the source to explain your answer. [8]

4 Study **Sources E** and **F**.
   Both sources are to do with anti-Vietnam War demonstrations held in Grosvenor Square, London, where the US embassy is situated. Do the sources agree with each other more than they disagree?
   Use the sources and your own knowledge to explain your answer. [7]

5 Study **Sources F** and **G**.
   How far does Source F challenge Source G about British students' commitment to political protest?
   Use the sources and your own knowledge to explain your answer. [7]

6 Use **all** the sources and your own knowledge.
   'British students were only playing at political protest.'
   How far would you agree with this statement?
   Use all the sources and your own knowledge to explain your answer. [12]

Index